The Semitic Secret

How Biblical Authors Organized Their Books
To Include Both a Dictionary/Commentary
And a Method to Disclose Scribal Errors

Robert W. North, Ph.D.

The Semitic Secret

*How Biblical Authors Organized Their Books
To Include Both a Dictionary/Commentary
And a Method to Disclose Scribal Errors*

Copyright © 2020 by Robert W. North

All rights reserved. No part of this book may be used or reproduced by any means, graphic, electronic, or mechanical, including photocopying, recording, taping or by any information storage retrieval system without the written permission of the publisher except in the case of brief quotations embodied in critical articles and reviews.

Because of the dynamic nature of the Internet, any Web addresses or links contained in this book may have changed since publication and may no longer be valid.

ISBN-978-0-9907795-8-2

7771—The Way of the Soul
www.7771.org
San Diego, California

Preface

Introduction

The Hebrews who composed the Bible and *The Gospel of Thomas* were Semitics, people who lived in the Middle East from at least 5,000 BC until today. Arabic and Hebrew are Semitic languages.

Most Semitic authors before 100 C.E composed and edited their works in their heads. They had limited writing materials if any. After completing their composition, he or someone who had memorized his work dictated it to a scribe. That copy would have been given to another scribe, sometimes years later, who copied it for the library of another person. Those copies became the "original" for further copies. That process continued for hundreds of years. As we can imagine, some scribes made mistakes. Other scribes cut out repetitive words and phrases to be more efficient. Further, a few scribes deliberately changed the text to agree with their or someone else's theology. So, the earliest manuscripts that we possess today includes hundreds of years of deliberate and chance modifications.

Our current translations of Semitic works are based on documents full of errors.[1] To make matters worse, translators imposed chapter, verse, paragraph, and phrase divisions that the authors of the texts did not put there. Stephen Linton, an Archbishop of Canterbury, developed the chapter divisions commonly used today around 1227 C.E. The Jewish rabbi, Nathan, divided the Old Testament into verses by in 1448 C.E.; and Robert Estienne divided the New Testament into verses in 1555 C.E.

These people imposed chapters and verses on the text for printing and reference purposes. Each later translator made sentence, paragraph, and phrase divisions according to his understanding of the material. Thus, each version of the Bible we view today is the result of the interpretations by people translating and laying out the text for publication. It is not what the Biblical and many other Semitic authors intended us to read.

---

[1] Ehrman, Bart D. *Misquoting Jesus*, Harper, San Francisco. 2005

The Discovery of Semitic Parallelism

Bible students have noticed that Semitic authors sometimes organized the text in patterns. For example, some people found arch[2] and other parallel arrangements.[3] No one, to my knowledge, has been able to discern the ancient literary principles and rules that the oral and written Semitic composers were following. For over 40 years, I passionately searched for them. My breakthrough in defining and learning how to use them came when I studied side by side *The Gospel of Mark* and the *Gospel of Thomas*, a pre-third century CE Semitic text. I found that their authors were using the same set of rules; although, both authors adapted them to their different literary forms. I called this ancient literary system, "Semitic Parallelism" (SP) because you understand the text by reading horizontally more than by reading vertically.

When I applied SP (Semitic Parallelism) to Semitic texts, I found:

1. That the Bible should not be laid out in newspaper columns like we see today. Instead, many, if not most, texts should be organized in columns consisting of three stanzas like you see on the front cover. We can find a notable exception to that arrangement in *The Gospel of Thomas*. The author of that work evolved Semitic Parallelism rules to create a unique book of highly organized, parallel wisdom poems.

2. That the Biblical authors organized their works to tell us their chapter and section breaks (which differ from those in our current Bibles).

3. That the organization of most texts discloses the authors' meanings for metaphors and sections, in other words, many Biblical and Semitic books contain an *internal dictionary and commentary.*

4. That we can determine where copyists have deleted and inserted text, as a result, *we can largely reconstruct the original document.*

5. That SP is a way for the authors to help their readers memorize their works. (Semitics possessed abilities that most today lack of begging able to memorize verbatim large quantities of text as someone recited them. Many could recall what we know today as the Old Testament.)[4]

---

[2] John Breck, *The Shape of Biblical Language,* Crestwood, N.Y., St. Vladimir's Seminary Press, 1994.

[3] Dennis Pardée, *Ugaritic and Hebrew Poetic Parallelism,* A Trial Cut, Brill, 1988.

[4] Achtemier, Paul J, "Omne verbum sonat: The New Testament and the Oral Environment of Late Western Antiq-uity." Journal of Biblical Literature 109, 1 (Spring 1990): 3-27.

Summary: The ancient Semitics developed a never-before-seen, unique form of literature that requires that people read it very differently than our current novels, newspapers, text books, poems, plays, etc.

Semitic Parallelism Implications

To understand the enormous implications of the discovery of SP, we might compare it to what many consider the most important archeological find ever—the translation of the Rosetta Stone.

Since about 200 CE, no one has been able to read ancient Egyptian hieroglyphics. Then, the Rosetta Stone, an Egyptian granite stele, was discovered in 1799. On it, the stone artisan inscribed the same message in hieroglyphics and Greek. Soon many people theorized that the Greek letters might equate to specific hieroglyphic symbols. If investigators could establish the equation, then we would be able to read hieroglyphic texts.

After about forty years, investigators were able to determine what Greek letter matched a specific hieroglyphic symbol. That led to people being able to read the hieroglyphic texts. In that way, the Rosetta Stone became the essential key to the modern understanding of ancient Egyptian literature and civilization.

The discovery of the translation of the Rosetta Stone is equivalent to the discovery of the principles and rules governing Semitic Parallelism (SP). In itself, it is a highly significant literary-archeological discovery. However, also, the use of SP has led to many other important archaeological finds. For example:

- When we read the Semitic texts such as the Bible according to SP, we understand the author's meanings. So far, in every document that I have analyzed, those meanings differ from most common interpretations, sometimes radically. That means that we need to question many of the conclusions of theologians, clergy, religious, and history scholars for the past 2000 years. We even need to examine archeological research results to the degree that the investigators have used Semitic texts to interpret their finds.

- Up until now, scholars have found that some sections of *The Gospel of Thomas* were organized around key words;[5] otherwise, the book appeared to be a casual

---

[5] Patterson, Stephen J., *The Gospel of Thomas and Jesus,* Polebridge Press, Sonoma, Ca, (1993), Ch. 3.

collection of sayings. In contrast, when I applied SP to the Gospel, I found that it is an intricately arranged 21-chapter book of wisdom poems. Further, because I could read it in a way that showed the author's meanings, I was able to discover his definitions for the metaphors. That, in turn, disclosed his main and sub-themes. All of those discoveries, then, led me to articulate fourteen reasons to believe that Jesus was the author.

- When I applied SP to the Bible, I understood that its authors taught two opposing ways to live. One was pro-indoctrination, especially the kind we find in religions. The second way was anti-indoctrination. It was taught by Abraham, Jesus, and other Biblical authors. In short, many of the Biblical authors were anti-religion.

All of these discoveries have been verified informally by my colleagues and editors. However, it will be many years before other scholars finish formally critiquing the findings. That leaves me with two choices: I could withhold publishing until the formal reviews have been completed, or I could publish immediately so that everyone can learn about, apply, and verify the SP and other sub-discoveries. I am choosing the latter course.

Further Information

To introduce SP to interested Bible students, I have published five books.

1. *The Semitic Secret*—this book. It is in two parts. The first part explains basic and intermediate SP rules as they apply to *The Gospel of Mark*. In the second part, I apply SP to many sections of the Bible and two sections of *The Gospel of Thomas*. I believe that this mass of evidence shows that in general, SP does disclose how many Semitic authors structured texts and left an internal dictionary and commentary.

2. *The Gospel of Thomas: In the Original 21 Chapter Arrangement.* I published the book in two ways: the "Standard Edition," which contains only 131 highly arranged wisdom poems and short appendices, and the "professional Edition" with extensive appendices.

   Semitic Parallelism reveals that The Gospel of Thomas is a 21-chapter, highly organized book of wisdom poems. This ancient methodology also discloses the meaning of the metaphors in the poems. With that information, I present in the Appendices 14 reasons to believe that Jesus was the author. Finally, In the Appendices to the *Professional Edition*, I use extensive examples from the *Gospel of Thomas* to explain the same Semitic Parallelism principles and rules that I teach differently in this book.

3. *The Second Coming of Eve, Abraham, Buddha, and Jesus—Their Lost Way to Personal and Global Peace.* In this book, I use SP to explain the meaning of these authors' metaphors, and with that information, how to understand their revolutionary, lost message.

4. *The Messiah's Unrealized Revolution Discovered in the Gospel of Thomas:* Few people seem to realize that no one, to my knowledge, can today explain Jesus' core message, which Mark describes as his "gospel of God" (Mk 1:14) and Luke, his "Way," (Acts 9:1-2). Many mistake it for the main tenants of Christianity, which are derived from the teachings of Paul the Apostle and later theologians.[6] In this book, I use SP to show that Jesus taught a theory of and a method for personal development. That was his mission. I contrast it with the theory and methodology of Paul the Apostle and of many Christian clergy today.

5. *The Gospel of Mark in its Original Dramatic Arrangement:* Today, this book is a draft. I used SP to organize the entire book. Check with our website www.7771.org to see when it is available.

Future publications and discussions by others and me will be published and indexed on my website www.7771.org. Anyone wishing periodic emails announcing new releases, announcements, and opportunities to join others in the discussion, may register on the site.

About Robert North

Robert North is a former member of the Society of Jesus (Jesuits). There he was educated in the classics, history, the humanities, and philosophy. After he left that order of priests and brothers, he earned a Ph.D. in Counseling at the University of Florida. While working in several colleges and universities, he continued the scripture scholarship that he began as a Jesuit. His focus has been on discovering the Semitic Principles used by the authors of the Bible and the Gospel of Thomas to organize their works.

---

[6] Wilson, Barrie, *How Jesus Became a Christian,* First St. Martin Press, 2009.

Contents

Preface iii

Chapter One: Semitic Parallelism Basics 1

Chapter Two: Semitic Parallelism and Allegories 27

Chapter Three: Advanced Semitic Parallelism Principles 39

Chapter Four: The Garden of Eden Allegory: Scene 1 59

Chapter Five: The Garden of Eden Allegory: Scene 2 65

Chapter Six: The Garden of Eden Allegory: Scene 3 67

Chapter Seven: The Garden of Eden Allegory: Scene 4 71

Chapter Eight: The Garden of Eden Allegory: Scene 5 75

Chapter Nine: The Garden of Eden Allegory: Scene 6 77

Chapter Ten: The Garden of Eden Allegory: Scene 7 81

Chapter Eleven: A Scene from the Gospel of Luke 85

Chapter Twelve: A Scene from the Gospel of Matthew 89

Chapter Thirteen: A Scene from the Gospel of John 93

Chapter Fourteen: The Covenant 97

Chapter Fifteen: A Scene from the Gospel of Thomas 103

Chapter Sixteen: Final Comments 107

Appendix: Act One of the Gospel of Mark 109

endnotes 134

Chapter One

Semitic Parallelism Basics

The Basic Grid

When we read a Bible today, we see that someone divided it into chapters and verses, with the verses arranged into vertical columns of paragraphs. We see some of those divisions below in a sample from a typical translation of MK 1:14-15:

Typical Arrangement of Mk 1:1-8

1 The beginning of the gospel of Jesus Christ, the Son of God. 2 As it has been written in Isaiah the prophet: "Behold, I send my messenger before your face who will prepare your way before you" 3 There came a voice, the one crying out in the wilderness: "Make ready the way of the Lord; make straight his paths."

4 There came John, the one baptizing in the wilderness, and he was preaching a baptism of repentance in order that one be released of his sins.

5 And all the Judean countryside and all of the Jerusalemites were going out to him. And they were baptized by him in the Jordan River. And they openly confessed their sins.

> 6 And there came John clothed with the hairs of a camel with a leather girdle about his loins, eating locusts and wild honey. 7 And he was preaching saying: "Comes the one stronger than me after me, of whom not I am sufficient having stooped to loosen the laces of his sandals. I baptized you with water, but he will baptize you with the holy spirit."

By using the Semitic principles and rules presented in this book, we know that Mark did not arrange the text in a column, as you see above. Instead, he organized that information in a 3 X 6 grid, as you see it below. (For now, ignore the "Act," "Scene," "Part" headings. I will explain these terms below).

Mk 1:1 Preface: The beginning of the gospel of Jesus Christ, the Son of God.[7]

Act 1, Scene 1, Part 1 Mk 1:2	Act 1, Scene 1, Part 2 Mk 1:3	Act 1, Scene 1, Part 3 Mk 1:4
Stanza 1	**Stanza 1**	**Stanza 1**
As it has been written in Isaiah the prophet: "Behold	There came a voice crying out in the wilderness:	There came John baptizing in the wilderness
Stanza 2	**Stanza 2**	**Stanza 2**
I send my messenger before your face	"Make ready the way of the Lord	And he was preaching a baptism of repentance
Stanza 3	**Stanza 3**	**Stanza 3**
Who will prepare your way."	Make straight his paths."	In order that one be released of his sins.

---

[7] The Preface: The beginning of the gospel of Jesus Christ, the Son of God. This Preface does not fit the structure of the Gospel. Further, Mark later calls Jesus' message, the "gospel of God," not the "gospel of Jesus Christ." And he does not address Jesus as "Jesus Christ." Thus, this we have evidence that this Preface was inserted by a scribe after Mark completed his work.

Semitic Parallelism Basics

Act 1, Scene 1, Part 4 Mk 1:5	Act 1, Scene 1, Part 5 Mk 1:6-7	Act 1, Scene 1, Part 6 Mk 1:8
Stanza 1	**Stanza 1**	**Stanza 1**
And were going out to him all the Judean countryside and all of the Jerusalemites	And there came John clothed with the hairs of a camel with a leather girdle about his loins eating locusts and wild honey	[Behold him,][8]
Stanza 2	**Stanza 2**	**Stanza 2**
And they were baptized by him in the Jordan River	And he was preaching saying: "Comes the one stronger than me after me	I baptized you with water
Stanza 3	**Stanza 3**	**Stanza 3**
And they openly confessed their sins	Of whom not I am sufficient having stooped to loosen the laces of his sandals."	But he will baptize you with the Holy Spirit."

---

[8] In this book, the brackets contain text that a copyist deleted after an author composed his original.

We see above that Mark organized the introduction to his gospel into six columns, each with three stanzas. This is the basic Semitic grid that we find in many works throughout the Bible from Genesis through Revelation. I demonstrate that by using SP to organize sections of the Bible in Chapters 4-14.

Jesus did not use this grid arrangement for *The Gospel of Thomas.* Instead, he modified SP ingeniously. I demonstrate his methodology in Chapter 15 and explain it thoroughly in the Appendices of my translation of *The Gospel of Thomas* (Professional Edition).

Parts, Scenes, and Acts

At the top of the grids of texts above, you see the words "Act," "Scene," and "Part." I call each chapter in Mark an "Act" because the Gospel, as you will see, is a dramatic allegory. I call each Act section a "Scene" to continue the dramatic vocabulary. I call each column a "Part."[9]

Suggestion:

To better conceptualize and analyze Act 1 of Mark, I suggest that you go to the Appendix and either cut out Act 1 or copy Act 1. Then, paperclip the pages together. In that way, you can remove pages and study them side by side.

Stanzas

A "stanza" consists of a subject and one transitive or intransitive verb.

When you read a Greek text of Mark, you will see that I sometimes translate a participle or gerund as a transitive or intransitive verb. On rare occasions, I translate a transitive or intransitive verb as a participle or gerund. Let me explain my reasoning:

After years of study, I concluded that the Semitic Parallelism system in the Bible demanded three stanzas in each part (column). However, if we use the current Greek or Hebrew texts, we sometimes identify more than three stanzas. That means that either the original author deliberately inserted an extra stanza (extra subjects combined with an extra transitive or intransitive verbs), or that a copyist over the past 2000 years inserted a stanza.

---

[9] Smith, Stephen H. (1995). "A Divine Tragedy: Some Observations on the Dramatic Structure of Mark's Gospel". *Novum Testamentum*. E.J. Brill, Leiden. **37** (3): 209–31.

Some of the cells in the chart of Scenes 1 and 2 appear to contain two stanzas. For example, Part 1, Cell 1, and Part 5, Cell 2 includes two stanzas. I do not know why, but I noticed in this *Gospel*, in other Biblical books, and in *The Gospel of Thomas*, that phrases and sentences that introduce a speech do not count as stanzas. In other words, when we read something like, "And Jesus said," or "The Lord God commanded," we are not to count those introductory sentences as a stanza.

After reading in parallel hundreds of Semitic poems, both in *Thomas* and in the Old and New Testaments of the Bible, I concluded that the authors probably intended that the subject be on one line and the verb on another. That construction showed that the subject needed to take responsibility for his decisions, which is a theme I found running throughout Semitic texts. Also, when we construe the stanza that way, we more easily see how the subject and verb of one poem parallel the subject and verb in a parallel stanza.

If the verb is copulative, it appears that the Semitic authors wanted the object to be on the next line. Repeatedly, I saw how that arrangement dramatically exposed the relationships within the parallels.

A single prepositional phrase after the verb works best on the same line as the verb. When one prepositional phrase follows another, the second seems to show parallelism best when placed on the next line.

When a strong qualifier follows a verb, such as "not," I found that such a word expressed more power and parallelism when put on the line after the verb.

Words and phrases before the subject seem to belong on lines above the subject.

Column Breaks

As you see, each column *usually* ends a complete thought that we punctuate with a semicolon or period. This rule applies the majority of the time. Often, what is a complete or punctuated thought to the Semitic author is not to me.

Further, a Semitic author must design the column breaks to fit other SP rules. I will explain those below.

Scene Breaks

Minor shifts in characters, mood, and setting indicate the beginning of a new scene. We will see that below at the end of Scenes 1, at the beginning and end of Scene 2, and at the beginning of Scene 3.

Act 1, Scene 1, Part 6 Mk 1:8	Act 1, Scene 2, Part 1 Mk 1:9-10	Act 1, Scene 2, Part 2 Mk 1:11-12	Act 1, Scene 2, Part 3 Mk 1:13	Act 1, Scene 3, Part 1 Mk 1:14
Stanza 1	**Stanza 1**	**Stanza 1**	**Stanza 1**	**Stanza 1**
[Behold him,]	And it occurred in those days that Jesus came from Nazareth of Galilee	And a voice occurred out of the heavens saying: "You are my son the loved	And he was in the wilderness for 40 days being tempted by Satan	And after the delivering up of John Jesus came into Galilee
Stanza 2	**Stanza 2**	**Stanza 2**	**Stanza 2**	**Stanza 2**
I baptized you with water	And he was baptized in the Jordan by John.	In you I am well pleased."	And he was with the wild beasts	And he preached the gospel of God
Stanza 3	**Stanza 3**	**Stanza 3**	**Stanza 3**	**Stanza 3**
But he will baptize you with the Holy Spirit."	And immediately going up out of the water he saw the heavens split and the spirit as a dove coming down on him.	And immediately his spirit thrust him out into the wilderness.	And the angels were serving him.	Saying: "The appointed time has been fulfilled

Notice the shift in characters and mood between Scene 1, Part 6, and Scene 2, Part 1. In Scene 1, John is the principal character. Jesus is that in Scene 2. The mood in Scene 1 is somber compared to the joy in Scene 2. The setting shifts again between Scenes 2 and 3. In Scene 2, Jesus is in the wilderness. In Scene 3, he is in Galilee.

Act Breaks

Major shifts in characters, mood, and setting indicate the beginning of a new Act. For example, there is a major shift in characters, setting, and mood between Mk 3:32-34 and 4:1. Mark 4:1 starts Act 2, as we see below.

Act 1, Scene 18, Part 1 Mk 3:31-32	Act 1, Scene 18, Part 2 Mk 3:32	Act 1, Scene 18, Part 3 Mk 3:33-34	Act 2, Scene 1, Part 1 Mk 4:1	Act 2, Scene 1, Part 2 Mk 4:2-3a
Stanza 1	**Stanza 1**	**Stanza 1**	**Stanza 1**	**Stanza 1**
And his mother and his brothers came	And a crowd was sitting about him	And Jesus answered them by saying: "Who is my mother and my brothers?"	And again he began to teach beside the sea	And the entire crowd was facing the sea upon the earth
Stanza 2	**Stanza 2**	**Stanza 2**	**Stanza 2**	**Stanza 2**
And they stood outside	And they chattered: "Behold your mother, and your brothers outside	And having looked around on the ones about him sitting in a circle he said: "Behold my mother and my brothers!	And a great crowd gathered to him	[And they listened to him;]
Stanza 3	**Stanza 3**	**Stanza 3**	**Stanza 3**	**Stanza 3**
And they sent in to him calling him.	And they are seeking you."	The one having done the will of God is my brother and sister and mother."	So he stepped into a boat to sit on the sea.	And he was teaching them in parables many things

I find 13 major shifts in *The Gospel of Mark*; and, thus, 13 Acts. Act 13 ends with Mk 16:8. There is additional material in our current Bible, but it does not fit the Gospel structure (shown below). That evidences that a copyist added the extra text after the author finalized the Gospel.

Horizontal Vocabulary

SP requires that the author use the same or similar words and phrases in a row of stanzas in a Scene.

For example, In Row 1 of Scenes 1 and 2, Mark uses the word "wilderness" three times and implies it a third time in Scene 1, Part 4. In Scene 1, Part 6, I inserted the word "wilderness" in a stanza that is missing. In another example, notice how many times Mark used the word "baptism" in Row 2 of Scenes 1 and 2.

Also, notice that Mark used the word "spirit" three times in Row 3. He also used a parallel word, "angel," as in one who delivers the message from the Spirit.

Some authors, such as Mark, repeat a word or action in a Row for the entire Act. For example, in Row 1, we find the words "come," "came," and "were going out" five times in the six Parts. Throughout Act 1 in Row 1, we will read the words "come," "came," and actions denoting the entrance of someone delivering a message.

Linguists will also discover that they will find the root or another part of a keyword in other words in a Row. You cannot see that in an English translation, but it is apparent in the Greek text of Mark.

Missing Text

In this book, brackets indicate that text is missing from our current Greek manuscript. See below:

Act 1, Scene 1, Part 3 Mk 1:4	Act 1, Scene 1, Part 4 Mk 1:5	Act 1, Scene 1, Part 5 Mk 1:6-7	Act 1, Scene 1, Part 6 Mk 1:8
Stanza 1	**Stanza 1**	**Stanza 1**	**Stanza 1**
There came John baptizing in the wilderness	And were going out to him all the Judean countryside and all of the Jerusalemites	And there came John clothed with the hairs of a camel with a leather girdle about his loins eating locusts and wild honey	[Behold him,]
Stanza 2	**Stanza 2**	**Stanza 2**	**Stanza 2**
And he was preaching a baptism of repentance	And they were baptized by him in the Jordan River	And he was preaching saying: "Comes the one stronger than me after me	I baptized you with water
Stanza 3	**Stanza 3**	**Stanza 3**	**Stanza 3**
So that one be released of his sins.	And they openly confessed their sins.	Of whom not I am sufficient having stooped to loosen the laces of his sandals."	But he will baptize you with the Holy Spirit."

You can see that in two cells in Scene 1, Part 6, I put text in brackets. We know that text is missing in Part 6, Cell 1, because there is no stanza where there should be one. In Part 6, Cell 2, the stanza needs an introduction, which I created by reading to the left in the row and copying another introduction.

So what you see in brackets is my reconstruction based on parallel words and phrases in the same row. My reconstruction of Part 6, Stanza 1, is a modification of Part 3, Stanza 1. My reconstruction of a section of Part 6, Stanza 2, repeats a section of Part 5, Stanza 2.

We can imagine a copyist of the original noticed that in Part 6, Mark repeated ideas that he said earlier. Because the copyist wanted to save time and parchment, and because he did not know Semitic Parallelism, he probably said to himself, "We won't lose any meaning if I leave out what Mark has said previously." Therefore, he skipped copying the text in brackets.

Translations

Current translators usually translate a given original word differently depending on the context and other parameters. One cannot do that and reveal parallelism. Instead, he must use the same translated word for the same word in the original. For example, I could not show that Mark used "erēmos" repeatedly in Row 1 if I translated it once as "wilderness," then as "desert," then as a "solitary, lonely, desolate place."

To increase the burden on the translator, he must use the same word and phrase when translating the original non-Semitic wisdom texts. For example, I revealed in my book, *The Second Coming of Eve, Abraham, Buddha, and Jesus* that Buddha and Jesus both employed the words "world," "darkness," "light," "life," and "death" to describe a person's character. It appears to me that many oral cultures used the same wisdom metaphors. Therefore, the translator must know more than the book in front of him. He also must be conversant with ancient wisdom literature in and outside the Bible.

Finally, a translator must also know the difference between the *Soul Way* and the *Mind Way*. I explained those two terms in my books, *The Second Coming of Eve, Abraham, Buddha, and Jesus*, and *The Messiah's Unrealized Revolution*. As I showed in those two books, Biblical authors primarily taught one way or the other.

If the translator does not practice the Soul Way, he may mistranslate the text. Mind Way thinking is so different that unless one lives on the Soul Way, he may not see parallels or the structure of the text. He also will not understand the meaning of Soul Way metaphors; therefore, he will not see their parallels in other phrases. For example, in *The Gospel of Thomas*, the word "twin" is parallel with the phrase "make the two the one," which is parallel to, "make her male." I have found that those parallels make perfect sense to someone on the Soul Way but not to many on the Mind Way.

Also, if a translator is not living on the Soul Way, he may not recognize division cues, such as between one Part and another.

To be clear: A translator of Semitic texts must:

1. Know Semitic Parallelism rules and principles,

2. Translate a given word in the original with the same word in every instance in the work in front of him and in other related Semitic and ancient texts,

3. Know the difference between the Soul Way and the Mind Way, and

4. Practice the Soul Way.

Row Parallels

When using SP, authors define words and phrases in parallel.

Literature today generally defines concepts in context, not in parallel. For example, a writer might say: "John the Baptist came into the wilderness. He was a holy man who lived in harsh conditions in order to abstain from anything that would distract him from giving his heart and soul to God. He called people to the live like him so that they could experience a life of stillness and oneness with God and the Torah Law, which is what they most deeply sought to be fulfilled."

Mark never defines a person, action, or concept like that. Let us look at how he defines John the Baptist.

Semitic Parallelism Basics

Act 1, Scene 1, Part 4 Mk 1:5	Act 1, Scene 1, Part 6 Mk 1:8	Act 1, Scene 2, Part 1 Mk 1:9-10	Act 1, Scene 2, Part 2 Mk 1:11-12	Act 1, Scene 2, Part 3 Mk 1:13
Stanza 1	**Stanza 1**	**Stanza 1**	**Stanza 1**	**Stanza 1**
And were going out to him all the Judean countryside and all of the Jerusalemites	[Behold him,]	And it occurred in those days that Jesus came from Nazareth of Galilee	And a voice occurred out of the heavens saying: "You are my son the loved	And he was in the wilderness for 40 days being tempted by Satan
Stanza 2	**Stanza 2**	**Stanza 2**	**Stanza 2**	**Stanza 2**
And they were baptized by him in the Jordan River	I baptized you with water	And he was baptized in the Jordan by John,	In you I am well pleased."	And he was with the wild beasts
Stanza 3	**Stanza 3**	**Stanza 3**	**Stanza 3**	**Stanza 3**
And they openly confessed their sins.	But he will baptize you with the Holy Spirit."	And immediately going up out of the water he saw the heavens split and the spirit as a dove coming down on him.	And immediately his spirit thrust him out into the wilderness.	And the angels were serving him.

Let us remember the rule: *When using SP, authors define words and phrases in parallel.* Therefore, we ask, "When we read Row 1, how does Mark define John?"

My answer: John is either a voice in the heavens, or he is Satan. Jesus, also, is either a voice in the heavens or he is Satan. Therefore, I conclude that John is the voice of Satan, and Jesus is the voice of God.

Let us consider Scene 5 to determine if we find more merit for this conclusion:

Act 1, Scene 5, Part 1 Mk 1:21-22	Act 1, Scene 5, Part 2 Mk 1:23-24	Act 1, Scene 5, Part 3 Mk 1:25-26	Act 1, Scene 5, Part 4 Mk 1:27a	Act 1, Scene 5, Part 5 Mk 1:27b-28
Stanza 1	**Stanza 1**	**Stanza 1**	**Stanza 1**	**Stanza 1**
And having entered Capernaum immediately on the Sabbath in the synagogue he was teaching	And immediately a man with an unclean spirit was in their synagogue crying out: "Do you want to destroy us Jesus of Nazareth?	And Jesus having rebuked it said: Be muzzled	And all in astonishment gathered together	[For when he rebukes them]
Stanza 2	**Stanza 2**	**Stanza 2**	**Stanza 2**	**Stanza 2**
And they were astounded by his teaching	I understand who you are.	And come forth out of him.	Saying: "What is this, a new teaching?	They obey him;"
Stanza 3	**Stanza 3**	**Stanza 3**	**Stanza 3**	**Stanza 3**
For he was teaching them with authority and not as the Scribes.	You are the holy one of God."	And the unclean spirit having convulsed him and having yelled with a great voice came forth out of him.	With authority he gives orders to the unclean spirits.	Therefore went forth his reputation immediately everywhere in the whole country around Galilee.

We might ask the following questions regarding Scene 5: "In Part 1, how does Mark define a synagogue and Jesus? In Part 2, how does Mark define the unclean spirit and Jesus? In Part 3, how does Mark define Jesus and his actions? In Part 4, how does Mark define "all" who are 'astonished?'"

My answer: In Part 1, the synagogue is parallel to the "wilderness;" therefore, to be in a synagogue is to be in the wilderness. In Part 1, Jesus is the voice of God.

In Part 2, the unclean spirit is the voice of Satan. Therefore, we know that John possesses an unclean spirit.

In Part 3, Jesus is the voice of God rebuking unclean spirits, including John.

In Part 4, unclean spirits fill the people who are in "astonishment."

Let us consider Act 1, Scene 18 and Act 2, Scene 1 to determine if our logic remains consistent:

Act 1, Scene 18, Part 1 Mk 3:31-32	Act 1, Scene 18, Part 2 Mk 3:32	Act 1, Scene 18, Part 3 Mk 3:33-34	Act 2, Scene 1, Part 1 Mk 4:1	Act 2, Scene 1, Part 2 Mk 4:2-3a
Stanza 1	**Stanza 1**	**Stanza 1**	**Stanza 1**	**Stanza 1**
And his mother and his brothers came	And a crowd was sitting about him	And Jesus answered them by saying: "Who is my mother and my brothers?"	And again he began to teach beside the sea	And the entire crowd was facing the sea upon the earth Stanza
Stanza 2	**Stanza 2**	**Stanza 2**	**Stanza 2**	**Stanza 2**
And they stood outside	And they chattered: "Behold your mother, and your brothers outside	And having looked around on the ones about him sitting in a circle he said: "Behold my mother and my brothers!	And a great crowd gathered to him	And he was teaching them in parables many things
Stanza 3	**Stanza 3**	**Stanza 3**	**Stanza 3**	**Stanza 3**
And they sent in to him calling him.	And they are seeking you."	The one having done the will of God is my brother and sister and mother."	So he stepped into a boat to sit on the sea.	[About how they may plant seeds of wisdom in their earth.].

Question: "Who are Jesus' mother and brothers?"

My answer: In Scene 18, Part 3, Jesus contrasts his mother and brothers with those who do the will of God. Therefore, his mother and brothers in Part 1 speak the voice of Satan.

Question: "What is important to Jesus' mother and brothers?"

My answer: Torah Law religion, the same thing that is important to John.

Question: "Where are Jesus' mother and brothers?"

My answer: They are "outside" the Kingdom in the wilderness living the spirit of Satan.

Question: Who in the Old Testament spoke the voice of Satan in the wilderness?

My answer: Mark wants us to remember that Moses died in the wilderness. He created Torah religion. Moses is a parallel figure to John and Jesus' mother and brothers and to anyone who preaches Torah Law religion.

In Act 2, Part 1, Mark describes Jesus as being "beside the sea" and "on the sea." He also describes the people as "facing the sea" and being on "dry earth."

Question: "What is the metaphorical meaning of the word "sea" and "dry earth?"

A clue: In Act 1, Scene 1, Part 4, Mark describes people in the Jordan River. Later in Act 1, Scene 2, Part 1, Jesus rises out of the Jordan, implying that the people remain in the river. The Jordan River is parallel to the "sea."

My answer: A "sea" or "river" in ancient times symbolized "emotions," and in Buddhist literature, "passions."[10] In Act 1, Scene 1, Part 4, Mark tells us that when the people did not rise out of the river, that is, they did not leave their emotional attachments to Torah religion.

In Scene 2, Part 1, John baptized Jesus in the Jordan. However, something radically different was cleansed out of Jesus. Mark tells us:

---

[10] I explain the meaning of "sea" and "Jordan River" with many examples in my book, The Second Coming of Eve, Abraham, Buddha, and Jesus.

> And immediately
> going up
> out of the water
> he
> saw the heavens
> split
> and
> the Spirit
> as a dove
> coming down
> upon him.
>
> And
> a voice
> occurred
> out of the heavens
> saying:
>
> "You
> are
> my son
> the loved
>
> In you
> I
> am
> well pleased."

Question: What is Mark telling us? Why did Jesus "go up out of the river" and John's followers did not? Why did the "Spirit as a dove" come down on Jesus and not on John and his followers? Why did the Voice in the heavens say about Jesus, "You are my son, in you, I am well pleased?" Why did not that Voice say that about John and his followers?

My answer: John and his followers remained trapped in their emotional (Jordan River) attachments to Torah-based religion. That is why they did not "go up out" of the river and why they were not "loved." Water baptism is for people to cleanse themselves of their sins that result from not following Torah religion laws.

On the other hand, when John baptized Jesus, he was inspired by the Spirit as a dove (messenger) to leave the guidance of Torah laws and be guided by no one and nothing but God.

Now we can better understand Jesus's statement where he tells us that his followers do the "will of God." Let us consider parallel Parts from Scene 1, 2, and 18.

Act 1, Scene 1, Part 6 Mk 1:8	Act 1, Scene 2, Part 1 Mk 1:9-10	Act 1, Scene 2, Part 2 Mk 1:11-12	Act 1, Scene 2, Part 3 Mk 1:13	Act 1, Scene 18, Part 3 Mk 3:33-34
Stanza 1	**Stanza 1**	**Stanza 1**	**Stanza 1**	**Stanza 1**
[Behold him,]	And it occurred in those days that Jesus came from Nazareth of Galilee	And a voice occurred out of the heavens saying: "You are my son the loved	And he was in the wilderness for 40 days being tempted by Satan	And Jesus answered them by saying: "Who is my mother and my brothers?"
Stanza 2	**Stanza 2**	**Stanza 2**	**Stanza 2**	**Stanza 2**
I baptized you with water	And he was baptized in the Jordan by John,	In you I am well pleased."	And he was with the wild beasts	And having looked around on the ones about him sitting in a circle he said: "Behold my mother and my brothers!
Stanza 3	**Stanza 3**	**Stanza 3**	**Stanza 3**	**Stanza 3**
But he will baptize you with the Holy Spirit."	And immediately going up out of the water he saw the heavens split and the Spirit as a dove coming down on him.	And immediately his spirit thrust him out into the wilderness.	And the angels were serving him.	The one having done the will of God is my brother and sister and mother."

Remember, "to repent" is to be baptized. Scene 1, Part 6 contrasts dramatically with Scene 2, Part 1 concerning repentance. In the second stanzas of both Parts, John baptizes with water. He intends that his followers and Jesus "repent" of not living the Torah law fully.[11]

However, when we read the second row horizontally, we learn that Jesus did not "repent" as John and his followers did. As a result, the Voice from the heavens said, "In you, I am well pleased."

So we ask, "Of what did Jesus repent that so pleased God?"

My answer: Jesus repented of allowing Torah-religion to guide him instead of the Holy Spirit. That is why he went "up out of the water" (emotional attachment to Torah Laws) and why he was rewarded with the "Spirit as a dove" coming down on him.

Mark teaches that no one else baptizes (cleanses) us. We baptize ourselves, depending on what we repent. Jesus repented of ever being divided from Spirit guidance. As a result, he was "loved," and the "angels served him" (Scene 2, Part 3, Stanza 3). "Angels" are a metaphor for "Spirit as a dove."

Question: "How does one do God's will" in every thought and action? (Scene 18, Part 3)?

Mark's answer: By not making the voice of Torah-religion more important than being directly guided by the Holy Spirit.

Back to Act 2, Scene 1: In Act 2, the crowd have left Torah religion and seek the voice of God in Jesus. We know that because they are on "dry earth" "facing the sea." To be on "dry earth" is to be without emotional attachments, which is necessary to listen to a radical message from someone speaking in oneness with the voice of God.[12]

Positive and Negative Parallels

In all of the rows, we find positive and negative parallel words and phrases. We have just seen that John, Jesus, God, and Satan are voices in the wilderness. The word "John" is

---

[11] This text is missing from the original. What is here is a possible reconstruction.

[12] Again, I explain the meaning of "dry earth" with many examples in my book, *The Second Coming of Eve, Abraham, Buddha, and Jesus*.

negatively parallel to the words "Jesus and "God" and positively parallel to the word "Satan." In another example, we saw that "synagogue" was positively parallel to "wilderness" and negatively parallel to "Kingdom." Further, we recognized that baptism in water is negatively parallel to baptism in the Spirit and to doing God's will.

Row Themes

Semitic Parallelism authors usually structure their texts to possess three rows. Each of those rows expresses a theme.

An SP rule: *The three rows generally express the following three underlying themes:*

Row 1 theme: *Condition for personal development.* The stanzas in this row may state the person in need of personal development, the person about to intervene, or in some cases, the stanzas may comment on the condition needed for personal development.

Row 2 theme: *The intervention necessary for personal development.* Stanzas in this row can also express the person or message delivering the intervention. In some cases, a stanza in the second row comments on the person, message, or nature of the intervention

Row 3 theme: *The result when a person develops or does not develop.* Stanzas in this row usually show how a person has become more alive or dead. The stanzas can also comment on the outcome of resisting or embracing the intervention.

We will look at parts from three scenes to verify that each possesses a three-stage underlying theme.

Act 1, Scene 1, Part 4 Mk 1:5	Act 1, Scene 2, Part 1 Mk 1:9-10	Act 1, Scene 3, Part 1 Mk 1:14	Act 1, Scene 3, Part 2 Mk 1:15	Act 1, Scene 5, Part 1 Mk 1:21-22
Stanza 1	**Stanza 1**	**Stanza 1**	**Stanza 1**	**Stanza 1**
And were going out to him all the Judean countryside and all of the Jerusalemites	And it occurred in those days that Jesus came from Nazareth of Galilee	And after the delivering up of John Jesus came into Galilee	And has drawn near the Kingdom of God;	And having entered Capernaum immediately on the Sabbath in the synagogue he was teaching
Stanza 2	**Stanza 2**	**Stanza 2**	**Stanza 2**	**Stanza 2**
And they were baptized by him in the Jordan River	And he was baptized in the Jordan by John,	And he preached the gospel of God	Repent	And they were astounded by his teaching
Stanza 3	**Stanza 3**	**Stanza 3**	**Stanza 3**	**Stanza 3**
And they openly confessed their sins.	And immediately going up out of the water he saw the heavens split and the spirit as a dove coming down on him.	Saying: "The appointed time has been fulfilled	And believe in the gospel."	For he was teaching them with authority and not as the Scribes.

In Scene 1, Part 4: The condition is the people going to John. The intervention is John baptizing. The result is their confession of their sins.

In Scene 2, Part 1: The condition is Jesus coming. The intervention is John's baptism. The result: Jesus rejected John's intervention and became more alive in the spirit.

In Scene 3, Part 1: The condition is Jesus coming again. The intervention is his preaching. The result is a statement about how one becomes more alive if he accepts the intervention—the gospel of God.

In Scene 3, Part 2 (this scene only has 2 parts): The condition: Being near someone like Jesus who lives the Kingdom of God. The intervention: Repenting of living Torah religion. The result: One believes not in the Torah Laws for guidance, but in the gospel of God, the foundation of which is living being guided by spirit.

In Scene 5, Part 1: The condition is Jesus entering the synagogue. The intervention is his teaching. The result is the unbelief of those who heard Jesus' teachings about the Kingdom.

Specific to *The Gospel of Mark*, the three themes in Act 1 are:

Row 1 theme: The voice of God or of Satan enters the lives of others.

Row 2 theme: People have the opportunity to be baptized (cleansed) by a ritual or by a teaching.

Row 3 theme: People become more or less in oneness with Spirit guidance and God's will.

Numbers

The Semitics found great significance in numbers. In SP, many elements are numbered. For example:

In Scene 1, there are six parts. Six is a symbol of imperfection, bad, and evil. So Mark tells us that Scene 1 that features John describes evil.

In Scene 2, we see 3 parts. Three is a symbol for a short period of time, or a short period of preparation. In Scene 2, we find Jesus preparing his ministry.

In Scene 3, we discover two parts. The word "two" represents two pillars at an entrance. In Scene 3, Jesus makes his entrance into the world.

I am not an expert in numerology; however, I tentatively consider Biblical numbers to mean the following: Number "one" means unity. Number "two" means "entrance" or the "beginning." Number "three" means "preparation" or "time of preparation." Number "four" seems to signify "wholeness" as in the four directions. Number "five" means strength as we find it in an arch. Number "seven" symbolizes perfection. Number "ten" appears to mean "power." (When a great force gathers, the Biblical authors often describe in it in multiples of 10. For example, a force of 10,000 is greater than one of 1000.) Number "twelve" seems to be a symbol for "strong-perfection" (adding five and seven).

Summary

We have just studied the basic SP rules and principles. With them, you can arrange much of the Bible and other Semitic texts as the authors intended.

As you probably noticed, the authors who employed SP created another genre of literature. We cannot read their works like our familiar novels, poems, textbooks, newspapers, blogs, and other narratives. We must understand their compositions according to their unique organization and logic.

Essentially, over centuries, the Semites invented a way to reduce a kilometer of information down to a centimeter of memorable text. We must remember that before 200 CE. most people could not read or write. Instead, they had to carry their library around in their minds. By using a structured framework that included rich metaphors and an internal dictionary and commentary, they created an ingenious literary form suitable for an oral culture.

Initially, one may be overwhelmed by the challenge of reading texts composed using SP; however, I discovered that with some effort and patience, their ancient method can be learned and enjoyed.

Chapter Two
Semitic Parallelism and Allegories

Introduction

Our use of SP has shown us some strange things in *The Gospel of Mark*. For example:

- We discovered that almost every important word and phrase is a metaphor for something else. People don't write that way today except in poems.

- We saw a God speaking to Jesus when he went up from the river in a manner so that others could hear the message. Does this happen to you?

- Later the Voice commented on Jesus' baptism. Who heard that voice? Only Jesus? If so, did he tell what he heard to others who passed it on to Mark? Or did others hear the Voice?

- Mark tells us that an unclean spirit was in that synagogue talking to Jesus. Have you ever seen such a spirit? Who saw this spirit and reported it to Mark?

- Mark says that Jesus "rebuked" the unclean spirit, and the spirit was "muzzled." That is a miracle, or can you do that? Again, how did Mark or anyone know that that happened?

- Mark describes Jesus meeting fishermen, apparently for the first time, and ordering them to follow him. They did, without any discussion and without consulting with their families. Is that realistic?

- Mark describes the encounter with the fishermen, Simon, Andrew, James, and John very differently than John, the evangelist, does in his gospel. Why do the two historical accounts differ so radically?

So we need to ask, "What kind of literature are we reading—a biography of Jesus, a history book, a fictional account of Jesus, a novel based loosely on some historical facts, what?"

The only answer possible: We are reading a unique type of *allegory*. For those unfamiliar with allegories, I offer the following overview.

Types of Allegories

An allegory is a narrative about one or more principal characters. The story consists of symbolic figures, actions, imagery, and events, which together create the moral, spiritual, or political meanings that the author wishes to convey.

An example is Homer's extended epic poem, *The Odyssey*. That work focuses on the Greek hero Odysseus, king of Ithaca, and his journey home after the fall of Troy. It is based loosely on historical events, which Homer changes to suit his primary purpose: to show how Odysseus both develops and declines in character as he encounters problems. As Homer does that, he teaches us how we might do the same in analogous situations.

In *The Odyssey*, as in most allegories, all the characters represent each of us in some way. Further, the animals and things in the story symbolize or are metaphors for aspects of ourselves. However, because Homer includes some facts that historians know happened, he composed a historical allegory, part history, part allegory.

In the Bible, we find some "pure allegories" with no historical facts. The Garden of Eden chapter in Genesis is an example. There are a few verses that tell of the physical location of the Garden; however, later in this book, we will see that the structure of the text shows that a copyist inserted the description of the rivers around the Garden (Gen 2:10-14) after the original was composed. Otherwise, there are no historical facts in the narrative.

In both pure allegories and historical allegories, the author intends *primarily* to show character development or decline, not history. Consequently, in a historical allegory, he may distort historical facts and invent things that never happened. That presents problems for historians and archaeologists when they try to research whether biblical events occurred, and conundrums for people who seek absolute truth in the *Bible*.

Mark, in his Gospel, had no intention of writing a true history of Jesus. In fact, as an allegory, the Book primarily is not about Jesus. He is a stand-in for each of us when we have become highly evolved in character. Mark intends that his allegory teach us how to become a Jesus.

We also are everyone in the Gospel. Sometimes we are a John preaching dogma, sometimes we are Satan or an unclean spirit to others, sometimes we are a disciple, and sometimes we hear the voice of God. Further, sometimes we baptize ourselves in water, and sometimes we do God's will by baptizing ourselves in the Spirit. Every metaphor describes some aspect of us and our lives. For example, we all must be psychologically crucified over and over to be a person of great character who saves the world from sin.

We know that the other New Testament gospels are allegories because the historical facts differ from one to the other. For example, in only the Gospels of Luke and Matthew, do we read about Jesus having a virgin birth. Jesus never mentions such a shockingly important event in any of his sayings and parables. Why? Because it never happened. In ancient times, a "virgin birth" was a metaphor for the birth of an exalted figure. In an allegory, an author is permitted to invent something and make it appear to be a historical fact. His main purpose, again, is to show character development or decline, not to write a historical narrative.

All of the Evangelists composed historical allegories. They describe some events that loosely or exactly match what happened. And they appear to quote Jesus, when in fact, sometimes they do, and sometimes they put their words in his mouth. We have no way to verify the accuracy of most of their narrations.

By using Semitic Parallelism, we recognize that much of the Bible consists of allegories. In my book, *The Second Coming of Eve, Abraham, Buddha, and Jesus*, I show that the early books of the Bible are largely allegories. I also demonstrate that these four authors used the same metaphors to convey the same meanings. That implies that in ancient times, allegories not only circulated throughout the world, but probably, everyone understood their key metaphors in the same way.

Because much of the Bible consists of allegories, unless we possess outside the Bible evidence, we must assume that most of what appears to be historical facts are the authors' inventions. The Bible is a book largely about each of us and our character development. It primarily is not about Abraham, Moses, King David, Jesus, and others as historical figures. Do we learn something about those people from reading the Bible? Perhaps, but we know little about their history. They are in the Bible as models for us in various stages of personal development.

Are there any truths in the Bible? Not absolute truths. Each of us interprets every word subjectively. For example, what the word "God" means to a given person is not what it means to anyone else. Further, what the word "God" means to a person yesterday may not be what it means to him today, especially when he evolves or devolves in character. When one has a dark day, he interprets everything, even a stop sign, differently than when in light.

The Biblical authors composed allegories to convey their understanding of character development. Then, they left it up to the reader to examine his life and decide if the allegory conveyed helpful truths.

Is there anything of value in the Bible. Of course! We can use the words of anyone to evolve in character.

Do we know what Jesus actually said? Yes, by reading *The Gospel of Thomas*. As I mentioned previously, in the professional version of my translation of the *Gospel*, I provide fourteen reasons to believe that Jesus composed it. Over 40% of the sayings in *The Gospel of Thomas* are in the New Testament, but all have been modified to some extent from what we read in *Thomas*.

Is there any reason to use the Bible rather than another book? Yes, many of the authors of the works in the Bible were very wise. It is usually better to listen to the wise rather than to the unwise.

Is it important to know historical facts about events and people in the Bible? Not for character development. For example, to know the exact year the Abraham lived or in what city Jesus lived does not help us to become more wisely loving of others. Or, in another example, people may receive comfort knowing that Jesus died on the cross for them; however, that remembrance does not automatically enable them to love as he did.

Allegory Generalization

We saw that a "wilderness" is a place where people are Satan controlled by the Torah Law. By reading Row 1 in parallel, we realized that Mark defined "Galilee" and a "synagogue" as wilderness places. We also saw how Jesus' mother and brothers were a wilderness family.

Those understandings of the meaning of the word "wilderness" are verified by its use in the Books of the Bible that describe Moses and his followers in the "wilderness." As I showed in my book, *The Second Coming of Eve, Abraham, Buddha, and Jesus*, Moses died in the wilderness outside of the Promised Land because he created a controlling religion that included the Ten Commandments and the Torah Law. The Promised Land is a metaphor for a highly evolved, fulfilled life. Jesus calls such a way of life, a "Kingdom." Joshua and the judges were able to enter into and live in the Promised Land (Kingdom) because they left controlling dogma, including the Torah laws.

Thus, the term "wilderness" in some parts of the Bible designates a place and people controlled by dogma-based religion. It is an internal and external darkness that is opposite the light that Jesus and others bring to the world.

Now, we need to ask, "What is a "wilderness" in our lives. We ask such a question because an allegory primarily is not about what was a "wilderness" in the past but rather, about how we might live now.

So to generalize Mark's allegory and its metaphors to today, we need to ask, "What was John doing and what was going on in a synagogue that applies to the life of anyone *no matter whether he is in or out of a religion?*"

John was indoctrinating people with dogmas. He was teaching them how to think and act. He also told them that God would both reward them for obeying his understanding of the Torah, and punish them when they did not conform to those laws. John was establishing a controlling cult with himself as its leader.

That is also what happened in the Synagogue. Clergy brainwashed people with answers to their personal questions. Those who conformed to the official ways to think and act were rewarded, and those who did not were punished or threatened with punishment.

Therefore, John and the clergy were teaching people to discriminate against others based on factors unimportant to whom they are as people. There is no difference between discrimination based on race, sex, wealth, and appearance and discrimination based on one's secular or religious faith. In Mark's words, discrimination is of Satan.

Therefore today, when we generalize the "wilderness" metaphor, we know that it is a place where leaders and their followers both indoctrinate others with their answers and teach them to discriminate against others who differ from the cult's norms. Such leaders can be ourselves, clergy, politicians, parents, the media, friends, or any other person whom we allow to control our thinking and behavior.

In his *Gospel*, Mark teaches his readers about both the danger of indoctrination and how to become independent by being guided only by the Spirit. That is what he means by being baptized (cleansed) in the Spirit. Or to put it another way, Mark was showing how Jesus guided people out of cults, not into them.

But remember, Jesus is a stand-in for each of us. So, Mark tells us that for us to be fulfilled and to be a savior of the world, we each also need to do two things: First, we must be a Jesus who grows in oneness with Spirit guidance. And second, we need to teach others how to make Spirit guidance more important than what they hear from authorities and friends. In other words, to be full of loving joy in the Kingdom, we need to leave our social cults and use Spirit guidance to become our independent real selves.

Mark also presents his solution for the resolution of religious and other dogma-based conflicts. He lifts up Jesus as a wise, great, independent, loving leader who led people out of social brainwashing to become like him and more. Because he did not identify with anyone's dogmas, he loved everyone just the way they were. In that way, he showed us that if we all do that, we will not conflict with others because they differed from us in theology, wealth, race, appearance, etc. In short, Mark's solution to inner and outer conflicts is: Leave divisive dogma-based organizations and become one with others. From that completely different lifestyle with its light rather than dark logic, we can wisely and efficiently work together to solve our practical problems.

Miracles in Allegories

Let us examine an example of parallel miracles in *The Gospel of Mark*. Below again is the organization of Act One. Notice that Scene 5 parallels Scene 14.

The Organization of Act One: 1:2-3:34

Scene 9 Mk 2:1-12b	←→	Scene 10 Mk 2:13-17
Scene 8 Mk 2:18-22	←→	Scene 11 Mk 2:23-28
Scene 7 Mk 1:35-39	←→	Scene 12 Mk 1:40-45b
Scene 6 Mk 1:29-34b	←→	Scene 13 Mk 3:1-6
Scene 5 Mk 1:21-28	←→	Scene 14 Mk 3:7-12
Scene 4 Mk 1:16-20	←→	Scene 15 Mk 3:13-19a
Scene 3 Mk 1:14-15	←→	Scene 16 Mk 3:19b-21
Scene 2 Mk 1:9-13	←→	Scene 17 Mk 3:22-29
Scene 1 Mk 1:2-8	←→ →←	Scene 18 Mk 3:31-34

Act 1, Scene 5, Part 1 Mk 1:21-22	Act 1, Scene 5, Part 2 Mk 1:23-24	Act 1, Scene 5, Part 3 Mk 1:25-26	Act 1, Scene 5, Part 4 Mk 1:27a	Act 1, Scene 5, Part 5 Mk 1:27b-28
Stanza 1	**Stanza 1**	**Stanza 1**	**Stanza 1**	**Stanza 1**
And having entered Capernaum immediately on the Sabbath in the synagogue he was teaching	And immediately a man with an unclean spirit was in their synagogue crying out: "Do you want to destroy us Jesus of Nazareth?	And Jesus having rebuked it said: Be muzzled	And all in astonishment gathered together	[For when he rebukes them by saying: Be muzzled"]
Stanza 2	**Stanza 2**	**Stanza 2**	**Stanza 2**	**Stanza 2**
And they were astounded by his teaching;	I understand who you are	And come forth out of him;	Saying: "What is this a new teaching?	They obey him;"
Stanza 3	**Stanza 3**	**Stanza 3**	**Stanza 3**	**Stanza 3**
For he was teaching them with authority and not as the Scribes.	You are the holy one of God."	And the unclean spirit having convulsed him and having yelled with a great voice came forth. out of him.	With authority he gives orders to the unclean spirits.	And therefore his reputation went forth immediately everywhere in the whole country around Galilee.

Act 1, Scene 14, Part 1 Mk 3:7-8	Act 1, Scene 14, Part 2 Mk 3:9	Act 1, Scene 14, Part 3 Mk 3:10	Act 1, Scene 14, Part 4 Mk 3:11	Act 1, Scene 14, Part 5 Mk 3:12
Stanza 1	**Stanza 1**	**Stanza 1**	**Stanza 1**	**Stanza 1**
And Jesus with his disciples withdrew to the sea	And he told his disciples that a little boat should constantly be serviceable to him	For he cured many	And the unclean spirits whenever they recognized him	[And because they recognized him]
Stanza 2	**Stanza 2**	**Stanza 2**	**Stanza 2**	**Stanza 2**
And a great multitude from the Galilee and from the Judea and from Jerusalem and from the Idumea and from the other side of the Jordan and from Tyre and Sidon after hearing the many things he is doing	In order that the crowd not press upon him	With the result that many with scourges were falling upon him	Fell down before him	He said many things in rebuke of them
Stanza 3	**Stanza 3**	**Stanza 3**	**Stanza 3**	**Stanza 3**
Came to him.	[And so that they not touch him inappropriately.]	So that he might touch them.	And cried out saying: "You are the son of God."	So that they should not make him manifest.

When we study Scenes 5 and 14 side-by-side, we notice many parallels. In both, there is a crowd of people who are amazed by Jesus' personal power. We also see in both scenes an unclean spirit, each of whom says roughly the same things: "You are the Holy One of God," and "You are the son of God." In both scenes, the mood is dark, hysterical, and adversarial. That is enough evidence for us to know that Mark designed the two scenes to be in an equivalent parallel relationship.

Let us examine the context. In Scene 5, Jesus and the crowd are in the Synagogue. Jesus speaks with the voice of God and the others with the voice of Satan. Because Scene 14 is parallel to Scene 5, we know that Mark wants us to understand that the sea context is dark wilderness also. Again Jesus is God's voice, and the crowd and unclean spirit are the voices of Satan.

Question: In both scenes, Mark introduces an "unclean spirit." So, we need to ask, "How does this evil one differ from the other hysterical people?

My answer: We find the answer when we examine what these spirits say: "You are the holy one of God," and "You are the son of God." The crowd does not shout those words because they do not see Jesus as the voice of God. Instead, they view Jesus as someone like them.

On the other hand, the unclean spirits see what Jesus was doing: calling people out of dark religious control and teaching them to use Spirit guidance to be themselves and to discover their own answers. These unclean spirits, therefore, face a choice—to remain unclean in the cult or to be baptized (cleaned) in the Spirit. They chose their former way of life. In other words, because unlike the crowd, they consciously decided not to be clean, they became Satan's full-throated evil voice in the world.

Question: Did these unclean spirits historically live?

My answer: Yes, and they live today in all of us when we consciously choose to be dogma controlled.

Question: In Scene 14, we see Jesus curing people of "scourges." What are they, and how does Jesus remove them?

My answer: In a dogma cult, we see ourselves as good and those who do not believe and follow our official doctrine as bad. Those judgments divide us from others. Instead of living in oneness, love, and peace with them, we experience them over against us. When conflicts arise, we may be tempted to be hatefully discriminatory.

When we see ourselves and good and others as bad, we also feel divided from ourselves. Instead of loving ourselves for who we are, we love ourselves for living the dogmas of others. That invites us to feel anger, guilt, fear, depression, and worried that we might be censored for not thinking and acting as expected.

All of those feelings and ideas that arise out of being divided from others and ourselves are the "scourges." In the Synagogue, Jesus heals such people by loving them as perfect, just the way they are.

Did Jesus historically work miracles? Possibly, but Mark is not saying that. Instead, he metaphorically shows him doing what we need to do to heal ourselves and others of scourges.

Conclusion

Mark composed a personal and group development allegory. In it, he describes us today as living in multi-layered cults in which officials and friends tell us how to think and act. He then tells us that Jesus' mission was to lead us out of our wildernesses by using Spirit to discover our own answers. In the course of doing that, Mark encourages each of us to be a Jesus who heals ourselves and the world of dogma-based "scourges."

Chapter Three

Advanced Semitic Parallelism Principles

First Level Parallel Columns

As we saw, Scene One consists of six parallel columns. That is what I call a first-level parallel column arrangement. Here it is again:

Act 1, Scene 1, Part 1 Mk 1:2	Act 1, Scene 1, Part 2 Mk 1:3	Act 1, Scene 1, Part 3 Mk 1:4	Act 1, Scene 1, Part 4 Mk 1:5	Act 1, Scene 1, Part 5 Mk 1:6-7	Act 1, Scene 1, Part 6 Mk 1:8
Stanza 1	**Stanza 1**	**Stanza 1**	**Stanza 1**	**Stanza 1**	**Stanza 1**
As it has been written in Isaiah the prophet: "Behold	There came a voice crying out in the wilderness:	There came John baptizing in the wilderness	And were going out to him all the Judean countryside and all of the Jerusalemites	And there came John clothed with the hairs of a camel with a leather girdle about his loins eating locusts and wild honey	[Behold him,]
Stanza 2	**Stanza 2**	**Stanza 2**	**Stanza 2**	**Stanza 2**	**Stanza 2**
I send my messenger before your face	"Make ready the way of the Lord	And he was preaching a baptism of repentance	And they were baptized by him in the Jordan River	And he was preaching saying: "Comes the one stronger than me after me	I baptized you with water
Stanza 3	**Stanza 3**	**Stanza 3**	**Stanza 3**	**Stanza 3**	**Stanza 3**
Who will prepare your way."	Make straight his paths."	So that one be released of his sins.	And they openly confessed their sins.	Of whom not I am sufficient having stooped to loosen the laces of his sandals."	But he will baptize you with the Holy Spirit."

Second Level Parallel Columns

According to SP, we should see scene one as two vertical parallel columns:

Part 3	←→	Part 4
Part 2	←→	Part 5
Part 1	←→	Part 6

Notice that Mark arranged the Parts so that we read up the first column and down the second. I have seen the reverse, where elements are arranged down the first column and up the second, but that organization seems to be rare.

The arrows indicate that the two columns are positively parallel. If they were negatively parallel, the arrows would look like this →← .

Let us read two of the columns according to SP rules:

Act 1, Scene 1, Part 3 Mk 1:4		Act 1, Scene 1, Part 4 Mk 1:5
Stanza 1		**Stanza 1**
John came baptizing in the wilderness	←→ The Condition–Result Parallel Relationship	And all the Judean countryside and all of the Jerusalemites were going out to him
Stanza 2		**Stanza 2**
And he was preaching a baptism of repentance	←→ The Anticipation–Fulfillment Parallel Relationship	And they were baptized by him in the Jordan River
Stanza 3		**Stanza 3**
So that one be released of his sins.	←→ The Anticipation–Fulfillment Parallel Relationship	And they openly confessed their sins.

In level one Parallel Columns, Parts 3 and 4 are parallel to Parts 1, 2, 5, and 6. In level two, Part 3 and 4 have a special parallel relationship.

The Semitics understood at least 12 kinds of parallel relationships:

1. The Equivalent Relationship (x = y)

2. The Opposed Relationship (x is opposite to or opposed to y)

3. The Analogous Relationship (x is similar to y)

4. The Anticipation–Fulfillment Relationship (x is a foreshadow of y)

5. The Prophesy–Fulfillment Relationship (x predicts y)

6. The Cause-Effect Relationship (x caused y)

7. The Statement–Example Relationship (x—in the abstract as shown by y in the concrete)

8. The Condition–Result Relationship (because x happened, y was able to happen)

9. The Beginning–End Relationship (x began it, and y ended it)

10. The First Stage–Later Stage Relationship (x began a series of events that resulted in y)

11. The Statement–Reason or Explanation Relationship (x is an abstract statement that the author explains in y)

12. The Event–Reason or Explanation Relationship (x happened because of this:).

Reconstructing the Original Text

We saw above how we can spot deleted text. By organizing the document according to SP, we can also tell when a copyist added text. We can see this in Act 1, Scene 4.

Act 1, Scene 4,
Part 1 Mk 1:16-18

And
passing by the sea
of Galilee
he
saw Simon
and Andrew,
the brother
of Simon,
casting their nets
into the sea

For
they
were
fishermen

And
he
said to them:

"Here
behind me

And
I
will make you
fishermen
of men;"

And immediately
having released the nets
they
followed him.

Act 1, Scene 4,
Part 2 Mk 1:19-20

And
stepping on a little
he
saw James
the son of Zebedee
and John
his brother
in the boat
mending their nets

And immediately
he
called them

And
after releasing their father
Zebedee
in the boat
with the hired men
they
went off behind him.

On the left is what is in our current text. Part 1 seems to contain five stanzas. Stanza 3 (And he said to them:) is an introductory announcement. As I explained above, it does not count as a stanza. Therefore, Part 1 contains five stanzas.

It is more likely that a copyist added the "fishermen" stanzas (stanzas 2 and 4) in Part 1 because:

1. All of the parts of this *Gospel* have three stanzas.

2. The stanza: "For they were fishermen" is not needed. Why else would these men be "casting their nets into the sea" if they were not fishermen?

3. The stanzas: "For they were fishermen" "And I will make you fishermen of men" do not parallel stanzas in Part 2. Further, they sound like something pious that a devoted Christian scribe might insert.

4. Finally, in this Gospel, Jesus never again refers to himself or his disciples as a "fishermen of men."

Therefore, Mark probably composed Act 1, Scene 4, as we see below:

Act 1, Scene 4, Part 1 Mk 1:16-18		Act 1, Scene 4, Part 2 Mk 1:19-20
Stanza 1	**Stanza 1**	**Stanza 1**
And passing by the sea of Galilee he saw Simon and Andrew, the brother of Simon, casting their nets into the sea	←→ The Equivalent Parallel Relationship	And stepping on a little he saw James the son of Zebedee and John his brother in the boat mending their nets
Stanza 2	**Stanza 2**	**Stanza 2**
And he said to them: "Here behind me;"	←→ The Statement– Explanation Parallel Relationship	And immediately he called them
Stanza 3	**Stanza 3**	**Stanza 3**
And immediately having released the nets they followed him.	←→ The Equivalent Parallel Relationship	And after releasing their father Zebedee in the boat with the hired men they went off behind him.

More Examples of the Two-Column Arrangement

Scenes, Acts, and Books can be organized in two columns. Below we see how Mark organized Act 1 in two columns.

The Organization of Act One: 1:2-3:34

Scene 9 Mk 2:1-12b	←→	Scene 10 Mk 2:13-17
Scene 8 Mk 2:18-22	←→	Scene 11 Mk 2:23-28
Scene 7 Mk 1:35-39	←→	Scene 12 Mk 1:40-45b
Scene 6 Mk 1:29-34b	←→	Scene 13 Mk 3:1-6
Scene 5 Mk 1:21-28	←→	Scene 14 Mk 3:7-12
Scene 4 Mk 1:16-20	←→	Scene 15 Mk 3:13-19a
Scene 3 Mk 1:14-15	←→	Scene 16 Mk 3:19b-21
Scene 2 Mk 1:9-13	←→	Scene 17 Mk 3:22-29
Scene 1 Mk 1:2-8	←→ →←	Scene 18 Mk 3:31-34

Scenes 1 and 18: As you can see above, Scene 1 is both positively and negatively parallel to Scene 18. John, in Scene 1, is positively parallel to Jesus' mother and brothers in Scene 18. Also, in Scene 1, John is negatively parallel to Jesus, and those doing God's will in Scene 18. There are many other signs that the two scenes possess an equivalent and an opposed relationship.

Scenes 4 and 15: We can easily recognize that Scenes 4 and 15 have a positive parallel relationship:

Act 1, Scene 4, Part 1 Mk 1:16-18	Act 1, Scene 4, Part 2 Mk 1:19-20	Act 1, Scene 15, Part 1 Mk 3:13	Act 1, Scene 15, Part 2 Mk 3:14-15	Act 1, Scene 15, Part 3 Mk 3:16-19a
Stanza 1	**Stanza 1**	**Stanza 1**	**Stanza 1**	**Stanza 1**
And passing by the sea of Galilee he saw Simon and Andrew the brother of Simon casting their nets into the sea	And stepping on a little he saw James the son of Zebedee and John his brother in the boat mending their nets	And after stepping up on the mountain he called to himself	And he made a group of twelve	And he made a group of twelve
Stanza 2	**Stanza 2**	**Stanza 2**	**Stanza 2**	**Stanza 2**
And he said to them: "Here behind me."	And immediately he called them	Whom he wanted	Whom he called "apostles"	And he called Simon[16] and James the son of Zebedee and John, the brother of James[17] and Andrew and Philip and Bartholomew and Matthew and Thomas and James the son of Alphaeus and Thaddaeus and Simon the Cananaean and Judas Iscariot

---

[13] *Simon:* After Simon in our current Greek text is the word "Peter" which seems to be a later insertion.

[14] *James:* After James in our current Greek text are the words "Boanerges or Sons of Thunder" which seems to be a later insertion.

Stanza 3	Stanza 3	Stanza 3	Stanza 3	Stanza 3
And immediately having released the nets they followed him.	And after releasing their father Zebedee in the boat with the hired men they went off behind him	And they went to him.	So that they might be with him to be sent off to preach and to throw out demons with authority.	Who also delivered him up.

In both Scene 4 and 15, Jesus calls his disciples. Therefore, the two Scenes possess an equivalent parallel relationship. When we read each row horizontally, we recognize that Mark used the same or similar words and phrases. That further provides evidence that the two Scenes are parallel.

The Arch Arrangement

Consider the stone arch below, which is the template for the literary organization that we find in Semitic literature.[15]

The arch above consists of five stones. The bottom stones on the left and the right are called "foundation stones." The middle wedged-shaped stone is called the "keystone."

---

[15] John Breck, *The Shape of Biblical Language*, Crestwood, N.Y., St. Vladimir's Seminary Press, 1994.

The arch was a significant early engineering invention. It enabled builders to span great distances with blocks of stone. The arch could support tremendous weight, and it gave walls with windows a sense of being light and, of course, it enabled doors on buildings to be wide, light, and beautiful.

For an arch to be strong, the left and right sides must be made of huge stones shaped to fit solidly on top of each other. Their weight must be sufficient to support horizontal and vertical pressures. The keystone is the most important unit of the arch. It must be strong and perfectly shaped to withstand the stress coming from all directions.

Bible students have long noticed the arch arrangement in Semitic literature. Some called it a "chiasmus." Others called an X arrangement of text a "chiasmus." The inconsistent use of the word "chiasmus" has led to confusion. Today, there seems to be no single accepted definition of it. Consequently, I use the term "arch" for this textual arrangement.

Let us look at Act 1, Scene 1, Part 3 in an arch:

Act 1, Scene 1, Part 3
Mk 1:4

Stanza 2

And
he
was preaching a baptism
of repentance

Stanza 1

John
came
baptizing
in the wilderness

← ↑ →

Stanza 3

So that
one
be released
of his sins.

Inherent Meaning of the Arch

In the arch above, Stanza 1 is the "condition" for making Stanzas 2 and 3 happen. Stanza 2 is the "intervention" into the lives of others. And Stanza 3 is the intended "result." The majority of arches in the Bible and other Semitic literature possess that three-stage underlying meaning. It outlines character development or decline, as we see below.

Stage Two (Keystone)

A person who speaks something to cause someone to develop or decline in character, or a word or phrase that does that, or an event that happens that does that.

Stage One (Left side)

The Condition for personal character development or decline

Stage Three (Right side)

What happens as a result of what happens in Stage 2.

We can see the three stage personal development/decline stages in two parallel arches below:

Act 1, Scene 1, Part 3, Mk 1:4				Act 1, Scene 1, Part 4, Mk 1:5		
	Stanza 2 And he was preaching a baptism of repentance **The Intervention**			**Stanza 2** And they were baptized by him in the Jordan River **The Intervention**	
Stanza 1 John came baptizing in the wilderness **The Condition**	← ↑ →	**Stanza 3** So that one be released of his sins. **The Result**	**Stanza 1** And all the Judean countryside and all of the Jerusalemites were going out to him **The Condition**	← ↑ →	**Stanza 3** And they openly confessed their sins. **The Result**

The entire Gospel is in a condition—intervention—result arch:

The Organization of *The Gospel of Mark*

	Act 7 Mk 11:1-33	
Act 6 Mk 8:22-26,[19] 10:13-50	←↑→	**Act 8** Mk 12:1-44
Act 5 Mk 8:27-9:42	←↑→	**Act 9** Mk 13:1-37
Act 4 Mk 6:14-8:21	←↑→	**Act 10** Mk 14:1-26
Act 3 Mk 4:35-6:1	←↑→	**Act 11** Mk 14:27-72
Act 2 Mk 4:1-34	←↑→	**Act 12** Mk 15:1-39
Act 1 Mk 1:1-3:34	←↑→	**Act 13** Mk 15:40-16:1-8

Acts 1-6 present Jesus' ministry—the condition. Act 7 describes Jesus entering Jerusalem on a donkey—the intervention. Acts 8-13 describe Jesus' arrest, trial, suffering, death, and burial—the result of the intervention.[16]

Not all arches express the condition—intervention—result dynamic. Below is a "definition" arch arrangement from *The Gospel of Thomas* (Saying 3):

---

[16] Mark 8:22-26 (Scene 1) is found at the end of Act 4 in our current text; however, it does not fit the Act 4 organization. But it fits perfectly here in the Act 6 organization. Mark 10:1-12 is found here in our current text. That scene does not fit the organization of Act 6; therefore, we know that a scribe inserted it.

Stanza 2

It
is
of your eye inward

Part 1 of the definition or explanation

Stanza 1

The kingdom:

The thing to be defined or explained

←↑→

Stanza 3

And
it
is
of your eye inward

Part 2 of the definition or explanation

In this arch structure, the "kingdom" is defined as an evolved way of third-eye seeing oneself and all.

Summary: The two most common Semitic arch arrangements that I have found are the developmental arch and the definition arch.

Additional Semitic Parallelism Principles and Rules

I found that some Semitic authors expanded on SP and used the regular system in creative ways. Jesus brilliantly did those things in *The Gospel of Thomas*.

In the NT gospels and in *The Gospel of Thomas*, we find 12 times a SP-arranged poem by Jesus. No other saying is repeated more than four times; consequently, we know that the following poem was the foundation of his "gospel of God" and his "Way:"

			1	*Seeking a fulfilled life:* This phrase is implied.
	Who has his ear to listen.²		2	*Who has his ear to listen:* Who has his third intuitive ear to listen directly to messages from God.
	Intervention			
He [seeking a fulfilled life]¹		Let him listen.³	3	*Let him listen:* I support his listening because that is my Way.
Condition		**Result**		

Condition: The "condition" to be on Jesus' Way is to be a seeker, not a steadfast believer.

Intervention: To obtain information directly from Spirit, one needs to use his intuition, not his two-ear analytic mind. So, one must develop his third ear to enable Spirit to *intervene* in one's life.

Result: As a result, one joins with others on the Way who are baptized in the Spirit.

As the foundation of Jesus' "Way," this poem does not tell people to embrace religious or any other kinds of beliefs. Instead, it encourages seekers to discover their own answers through the guidance of Spirit. Therefore, this poem supports Mark's understanding of Jesus' gospel and Way.

In *The Gospel of Thomas*, Jesus composes arch-arranged poems with five and seven stanzas such as the following two-part poem (Saying 3b):

Part 1				Part 2		
	Stanza 3 And you will realize				**Stanza 2** Then you exist in poverty	
Stanza 2 Then they will know you	←↑→	**Stanza 4** That you are sons of the Father	←→ An Opposed Relationship	**Stanza 1** If you will know yourselves not	←↑→	**Stanza 3** And you are the poverty.
Stanza 1 When you should know yourselves	←↑→	**Stanza 5** Who lives.				

In Part One of the above poem, Jesus states that he and everyone else is the son or daughter of the Father. However, they will only know and live that to the degree that they know themselves.

In Part Two, Jesus describes a person who does not know himself as living in inward poverty, and as being poverty outwardly in the world. One is poverty to the degree that one has poor knowledge of oneself.

Notice in Part One, that we can, with slight modifications, make a sentence out of parallel parts. For example, we could read Stanza 1 and 5 as "When you should know yourselves, you live." In another example, we could form Stanza 2 and 4 in a sentence by saying, "They will know that you are the sons of the Father."

Also notice two things about the parts: First, Part 1 is a condition-intervention-result arch, and Part 2 is a definition arch. Second, the two parts are in opposition.

Further Information:

I explain and give examples of *even more advanced* SP principles and rules in the many appendices at the end of my "Professional Version" of my translation and organization of *The Gospel of Thomas*. By registering on our site (www.7771.0rg), you can indicate if you want periodic emails that explain further SP discoveries.

Chapter Four

The Garden of Eden Allegory: Scene 1

Introduction

Up until this point in the book, I have both explained SP principles and rules and showed how they reveal the structure of Semitic texts. In this second section of the book, I will present exercises that will enable you to practice SP.

If you do the exercises, you will need paper, tape, and scissors. If you want just to read the results of the exercises, you will not need those things.

Exercise

On this page and the next is a text from the Garden of Eden Allegory. Take the pages to a copy machine and make a copy that you will cut up.

Genesis 2:4b-15

2:4b The day Being-Gods[17] made the earth and the heavens,
2:5 before a plant of the field was in the earth and before an
herb of the field had grown; for Being-Gods had not rained

---

[17] *Being-Gods:* The Hebrew text reads "Yĕhovah 'Elohiym." Those words are difficult to translate. "Yĕhovah" can be rendered as "Being." "'Elohiym" is plural and it means "Gods."

upon the earth, and there was not a person[18] to till the land, 2:6 and there went up a mist from the earth, and it watered the face of the land. 2:7 Being-Gods formed a person of the dust of the land and breathed into the nostrils the breath of life, and the person became a living being. 2:8 Being-Gods planted a garden to the east of Eden and put the person in it, whom that One formed. 2:9 Out of the land, Being-Gods grew trees compelling to see and good for food, [one was] the Tree of [the Knowledge] of Life in the middle of the Garden, and [the other was] the Tree of the Knowledge of Good and Bad. 2:10 And a river went out of Eden to water the Garden, and it parted and became four heads. 2:11 The name of the first is Pison, which surrounded the earth of Havilah where there is gold. 2:12 And the gold of that land is good: there are bdellium and the onyx stone. 2:13 And the name of the second river is Gihon, which surrounds the earth of Ethiopia. 2:14 And the third river is Hiddekel that goes toward the East of Assyria. And the fourth river is the Euphrates. 2:15 Being-Gods took the person and put that one into the Garden of Eden to till it and [that one was also] to guard it.

1. Using Semitic Parallelism principles, divide the text into parts (columns) and stanzas.

2. Tape the parts (columns) of stanzas beside each other on the typing paper. Place the stanzas in parallel rows

3. After you have done that, compare your organizational findings with mine below.

---

[18] *Person:* The Hebrew word "adam" can mean "person," "man," or "mankind." At this point, it means "person." We do not know if the person is a man or woman.

Problems

You were not able to able to determine the structure of that section because a copyist inserted text after the author completed the original. Therefore, read through the verses and look for a block of text that does not fit the structure both because it conveys a different theme and tone and because it of words not found in the other parts. After you have found the insertion, look at my answer below.

A copyist inserted the following text after the author completed his composition.

Genesis 2: 10-14

> 2:10 And a river went out of Eden to water the Garden, and it parted and became four heads. 2:11 The name of the first is Pison, which surrounded the earth of Havilah where there is gold. 2:12 And the gold of that land is good: there are bdellium and the onyx stone. 2:13 And the name of the second river is Gihon, which surrounds the earth of Ethiopia. 2:14 And the third river is Hiddekel that goes toward the East of Assyria. And the fourth river is the Euphrates.

1. Remove the above text.

2. Using Semitic Parallelism principles, divide the text into parts (columns) and stanzas.

3. Tape the parts (columns) of stanzas beside each other on the typing paper. Place the stanzas in parallel rows

4. After you have done that, compare your organizational findings with mine below.

Scene 1, Part 1 Gen 2:4b-5a	Scene 1, Part 2 Gen 2:5b	Scene 1, Part 3 Gen 2:6	Scene 1, Part 4 Gen. 2:7	Scene 1, Part 5 Gen. 2:8	Scene 1, Part 6 Gen. 2:9	Scene 1, Part 7 Gen. 2:15
Stanza 1	**Stanza 1**	**Stanza 1**	**Stanza 1**	**Stanza 1**	**Stanza 1**	**Stanza 1**
The day Being-Gods made the earth and the heavens	For Being-Gods had not rained upon the earth	[Being-Gods commanded]	Being-Gods formed a person of dust of the land	Being-Gods planted a garden to the east of Eden	Out of the land Being-Gods grew trees compelling to see and good for food	Being-Gods took the person
Stanza 2	**Stanza 2**	**Stanza 2**	**Stanza 2**	**Stanza 2**	**Stanza 2**	**Stanza 2**
Before a plant of the field was in the earth	And there was not a person to till the land	And there went up a mist from the earth	And breathed into the nostrils the breath of life	And put the person in it	[One was] the Tree of [the Knowledge of] Life in the middle of the Garden,	And put that one into the Garden of Eden to till it
Stanza 3	**Stanza 3**	**Stanza 3**	**Stanza 3**	**Stanza 3**	**Stanza 3**	**Stanza 3**
And before an herb of the field had grown	[And there was not a person to guard it].	And it watered the face of the land.	And the person became a living being.	Whom that One formed.	And [the other was] the Tree of the Knowledge of Good and Bad.	And [he was] to guard it.

Quiz

In Part 1, what is the "plant," and what is the "herb?"

My answer: the parallel stanzas in Part 6 tell us that the "plant" is the Tree of the Knowledge of Life, and the "herb" is the Tree of the Knowledge of Good and Bad.

Chapter Five

The Garden of Eden Allegory: Scene 2

Exercise

Copy the text below.

Genesis 2:16-17

> 2:16 Being-Gods commanded the person: Of the [fruit] of the Tree [of the Knowledge of Life] in the Garden, [you take and you] eat and eat. 2:17 Of the Tree of the Knowledge of Good and Bad, [you take and you] do not eat [and eat]. For on the day you eat of it, you will die and die.

1. Using Semitic Parallelism principles, divide the above text into parts (columns) and stanzas.

2. Tape the parts (columns) of stanzas beside each other on the typing paper. Place the stanzas in parallel rows

3. After you have done that, compare your organizational findings with mine below:

Scene 2, Part 1 Gen 2:16	Scene 2, Part 2 Gen 2:17a	Scene 2, Part 3 Gen 2:17b
Stanza 1	**Stanza 1**	**Stanza 1**
Being-Gods commanded the person: Of the fruit of the Tree of the Knowledge of Life in the Garden you take,	Of the tree of the knowledge of good and bad, you take,	For on the day you eat of it,
Stanza 2	**Stanza 2**	**Stanza 2**
And you eat	And you do not eat	You will die
Stanza 3	**Stanza 3**	**Stanza 3**
And eat;	[And eat;]	And die.

Chapter Six
The Garden of Eden Allegory: Scene 3

Exercise

Copy the text below.

Genesis 2:18-25

2:18 Being-Gods said: It is not good that the man[19] is alone; therefore I will make a helper in front of him. 19 Therefore, of the land Being-Gods formed living beings of the field and birds of heaven and brought them to the person to see what he would call them, for whatever the person called the living being, that was its name. 20 The person gave names to the beasts, to the birds of heaven and to living beings of the field, but for the man [who is alone] there was not found a helper. 21 So Being-Gods caused a deep trance to fall on the man as he slept and that one took one of the ribs and closed up the flesh. 22 Then Being-Gods made a woman from the rib which that One had taken from the man and brought her to the person. 23 And the person said: "This now is bone of my bones and flesh of my flesh; she shall be called woman because she was taken out of man." 24 Therefore a man will leave his father and his mother and will join to his wife, and they will be one flesh. 25 And they were both naked, the man [who is with] the woman, and they were not ashamed.

---

[19] As I explained in *The Second Coming* Book, adam means person, or man. In this scene, often it means both. You may disagree with my choice for the context.

1. Using Semitic Parallelism principles, divide the above text into parts (columns) and stanzas.

2. Tape the parts (columns) of stanzas beside each other on the typing paper. Place the stanzas in parallel rows

3. After you have done that, compare your organizational findings with mine below:

Scene 3, Part 1 Gen 2:18	Scene 3, Part 2 Gen 2:19a	Scene 3, Part 3 Gen 2:19b-20	Scene 3, Part 4 Gen 2:21
Stanza 1	**Stanza 1**	**Stanza 1**	**Stanza 1**
Being-Gods said: It Is not good	Therefore, of the land Being-Gods formed living beings of the field and birds of heaven and brought them to the person[27]	The person gave names to the beasts, to the birds of heaven and to living beings of the field	So Being-Gods caused a deep trance to fall on the man[28]
Stanza 2	**Stanza 2**	**Stanza 2**	**Stanza 2**
That the man is alone	For whatever the person called the living being,	But for the man [who is alone]	And that One took one of the ribs
Stanza 3	**Stanza 3**	**Stanza 3**	**Stanza 3**
Therefore I will make a helper in front of him.	That was its name.	There was not found a helper.	And closed up the flesh.

---

[20] *To see what he would call them:* This is in our current text, but it an insertion. It is the fourth stanza in this column. It is not needed.

[21] Our current text inserts here: "And as he slept." Because those words do not fit the structure, they were probably inserted by an early scribe.

Scene 3, Part 5 Gen 2:22	Scene 3, Part 6 Gen 2:23	Scene 3, Part 7 Gen 2:25
Stanza 1	**Stanza 1**	**Stanza 1**
Then Being-Gods made a woman from the rib	And the person said: This now is bone of my bones and flesh of my flesh	And they were both naked,
Stanza 2	**Stanza 2**	**Stanza 2**
Which that One had taken from the man	She shall be called woman	The man [who is with] the woman,
Stanza 3	**Stanza 3**	**Stanza 3**
And brought her to the person.	Because she was taken out of man.[29]	And they were not ashamed.

---

[22] *Gen 2:24:* Our current text inserts here: "For this reason, a man shall leave his father and his mother and join with his woman and they will become one flesh." Because those words do not fit the Scene structure which almost certainly is seven parts, and because the language and tone does not fit this Scene, or for that matter, the entire Allegory, this saying was probably inserted by an early scribe.

Chapter Seven
The Garden of Eden Allegory: Scene 4

Exercise

Copy the text below.

Genesis 3:1-25

1 The snake was more shrewd than any living being of the field which Being-Gods had made. He said to the woman: "Indeed God said, 'You may eat of the trees of the garden.'" 2 And the woman said to the snake: "From the fruit of the trees of the garden we may eat; 3 however of the fruit of the tree not in the middle of the garden the Gods said: 'You shall not eat of it or touch it, or you will die.'" 4 The snake said to the woman: "You will not die and die, 5 for the Gods know that on the day that you eat of it, your eyes will be opened and you will be Gods knowing good and evil. 6 So when the woman saw that the tree was good for food, compelling to the eyes, and a tree to be desired for wisdom, she took its fruit and ate it and she gave it also to her man, and he ate it. 7 Then the eyes of both were opened, and they knew their nakedness; therefore, by sewing fig leaves together, they made themselves aprons.

1. Using Semitic Parallelism principles, divide the above text into parts (columns) and stanzas.
2. Tape the parts (columns) of stanzas beside each other on the typing paper. Place the stanzas in parallel rows
3. After you have done that, compare your organizational findings with mine below:

Scene 4, Part 1 Gen 3:1	Scene 4, Part 2 Gen 3:2-3	Scene 4, Part 3 Gen 3:4-5a	Scene 4, Part 4 Gen 3:5b
Stanza 1	**Stanza 1**	**Stanza 1**	**Stanza 1**
The snake was more shrewd than any living being of the field	And the woman said to the snake: "From the fruit of the trees of the garden we may eat	The snake said to the woman: You will not die	That on the day that you eat of it,
Stanza 2	**Stanza 2**	**Stanza 2**	**Stanza 2**
Which Being-Gods had made.	However of the fruit of the tree not[30] in the middle of the garden the Gods said: You shall not eat of it[31]	And die	Your eyes will be opened
Stanza 3	**Stanza 3**	**Stanza 3**	**Stanza 3**
He said to the woman: "Indeed God said 'You may eat of the trees of the garden.'"	Or you will die.	For the Gods know	And you will be Gods knowing good and evil.

---

[23] *Not:* This word is missing from our current text. Without it, the stanza makes no sense because Being-Gods told the man the opposite previously: to eat of the tree in the middle of the Garden.

[24] Our current text inserts here: "Or touch it." Because those words do not fit the structure and because Being-Gods did not mention touching, they were probably inserted by an early scribe.

Scene 4, Part 5 Gen 3:6a	Scene 4, Part 6 Gen 2:6b	Scene 4, Part 7 Gen 2:7
Stanza 1	**Stanza 1**	**Stanza 1**
So when the woman saw	And ate it	Then the eyes of both were opened
Stanza 2	**Stanza 2**	**Stanza 2**
That the tree was good for food, compelling to the eyes, and a tree to be desired for wisdom	And she gave it also to her man	And they knew their nakedness
Stanza 3	**Stanza 3**	**Stanza 3**
She took its fruit	And he ate it.	Therefore, by sewing fig leaves together they made themselves aprons.

Chapter Eight

The Garden of Eden Allegory: Scene 5

Exercise

Copy the text below.

Genesis 3:8-13

> They heard the voice of Being-Gods as that one walked in the Garden in the cool of the day. So the man and the woman hid themselves from the face of Being-Gods among the trees of the Garden. Being-Gods called to the man and asked: "Where are you?" He said: "I heard your voice in the Garden, so being afraid and naked, I hid." Being-Gods asked: "Who revealed your nakedness? Did you eat of the tree of which I commanded you not to eat?" The man said: "The woman you gave me, she gave me of the tree, and I ate it." Being-Gods asked the woman: "What did you do?" The woman said: "The snake deceived me, and I ate it."

1. Using Semitic Parallelism principles, divide the above text into parts (columns) and stanzas.

2. Tape the parts (columns) of stanzas beside each other on the typing paper. Place the stanzas in parallel rows

3. After you have done that, compare your organizational findings with mine below:

Scene 5, Part 1 Gen 3:8	Scene 5, Part 2 Gen 3:9-10	Scene 5, Part 3 Gen 3:11	Scene 5, Part 4 Gen 3:12	Scene 5, Part 5 Gen 3:13
Stanza 1	**Stanza 1**	**Stanza 1**	**Stanza 1**	**Stanza 1**
They heard the voice of Being-Gods	Being-Gods called to the man and asked: "Where are you?"	Being-Gods asked: "Who revealed your nakedness?	The man said: "The woman you gave me	Being-Gods asked the woman: "What did you do?"
Stanza 2	**Stanza 2**	**Stanza 2**	**Stanza 2**	**Stanza 2**
As that one walked in the Garden in the cool of the day	He said: "I heard your voice in the Garden	Did you eat of the tree	She gave me of the tree	The woman said: "The snake deceived me
Stanza 3	**Stanza 3**	**Stanza 3**	**Stanza 3**	**Stanza 3**
So the man and the woman hid themselves from the face of Being-Gods among the trees of the Garden.	So being afraid and naked I hid myself."	Of which I commanded you not to eat?"	And I ate it."	And I ate it."

Chapter Nine

The Garden of Eden Allegory: Scene 6

Exercise

Copy the text on this and the next page.

Genesis 3:14-19

3:14 Being-Gods said to the snake: "Because you did this, you are cursed more than every animal and more than every living being of the field[25] and dust you will eat all the days of your life. 15 I will put hostility between you and the woman and between her descendants and your descendants; therefore, she will bruise your head, and you will strike her heel." 16 To the woman Being Gods said: "I will multiply greatly your sorrow in pregnancy; in pain you shall bring forth children, and your desire will be for the man to rule you." 17 To the man, Being-Gods said: "You have listened to the voice of the woman, and having eaten of the tree of which I commanded saying: "Do not eat of it,' of the cursed land sorrowfully eat all the days of your life. 18 It will grow thorns and thistles, and you shall eat the herb of the field. 19 And in the sweat of your face, you will

---

[25] Our current text inserts here: "On your belly you shall go." Because those words do not fit the structure, and because they do not make sense (was the snake hopping around on its tail or on legs before?), they were probably inserted by an early scribe.

eat bread until you return to the land 19 Until you return to
the land of which you were taken. [This is your fate] for you
are dust, and you will return to dust."[26,27]

1. Using Semitic Parallelism principles, divide the above text into parts (columns) and stanzas.

2. Tape the parts (columns) of stanzas beside each other on the typing paper. Place the stanzas in parallel rows

3. After you have done that, compare your organizational findings with mine below:

---

[26] Our current text inserts here 3:20: "And the man called the woman's name 'Eve,' because she was the mother of all living beings." Because this sentence does not fit the structure, because it does not fit the Scene theme which is punishment for disobeying, and because the man has already named her "woman" and not "Eve," it was probably inserted by an early scribe. Thus, no one in the Garden of Eden Allegory is named Adam or Eve.

[27] Our current text inserts here 3:21: "For the man and the woman Being-Gods made coats of skins and clothed them." Because this sentence does not fit the structure, because it does not fit the Scene theme, and because the man and woman already put on garments, this sentence was probably inserted by an early scribe.

The Garden of Eden Allegory: Scene 6

Scene 6, Part 1 Gen 3:14	Scene 6, Part 2 Gen 3:15	Scene 6, Part 3 Gen 3:16	Scene 6, Part 4 Gen 3:17a
Stanza 1	**Stanza 1**	**Stanza 1**	**Stanza 1**
Being-Gods said to the snake: "Because you did this	I will put hostility between you and the woman and between her descendants and your descendants;	To the woman Being-Gods said: "I will multiply greatly your sorrow in pregnancy,	To the man Being-Gods said: "You have listened to the voice of the woman.
Stanza 2	**Stanza 2**	**Stanza 2**	**Stanza 2**
You are cursed more than every animal and more than every living being of the field	Therefore she will strike your head	In pain you shall bring forth children	And you have eaten of the tree
Stanza 3	**Stanza 3**	**Stanza 3**	**Stanza 3**
And dust you will eat all the days of your life.	And you will strike her heel."	And your desire will be for the man to rule you."	Of which I commanded saying: 'Do not eat of it.

Scene 6, Part 5 Gen 3:17b-18	Scene 6, Part 6 Gen 3:19a	Scene 6, Part 7 Gen 3:19b
Stanza 1	**Stanza 1**	**Stanza 1**
Therefore, of the cursed land sorrowfully eat all the days of your life	And in the sweat of your face you will eat bread	[This is your fate][35]
Stanza 2	**Stanza 2**	**Stanza 2**
For it will grow thorns and thistles	Until you return to the land	For you are dust
Stanza 3	**Stanza 3**	**Stanza 3**
And you shall eat of the herb of the field.	Of which you were taken.	And you will return to dust."[36,37]

---

[28] In our current text, this stanza is missing. What you see is my reconstruction:

[29] Our current text inserts here 3:20: "And the man called the woman's name 'Eve,' because she was the mother of all living beings." Because this sentence does not fit the structure, because it does not fit the Scene theme which is punishment for disobeying, and because the man has already named her "woman" and not "Eve," it was inserted by an early scribe. Thus, no one in the Garden of Eden Allegory is named Adam or Eve.

[30] Our current text inserts here 3:21: "For the man and the woman Being-Gods made coats of skins and clothed them." Because this sentence does not fit the structure, because it does not fit the Scene theme, and because the man and woman already put on garments, this sentence was inserted by an early scribe. It is apparent that the scribe went to the end of the Scene and inserted 3:20-21.

Chapter Ten
The Garden of Eden Allegory: Scene 7

Exercise

Copy the text below.

Genesis 3:8-13

> 3:22 Being-Gods said: "Behold, the man has become one of us because he knows good and bad. Now lest he reaches out his hand to also take of the Tree of Life and eat and live forever, 23 Being-Gods sent him out of the Garden of Eden so that he till the land from which he was taken. 24 So, Being-Gods drove the man out and at the east of the Garden of Eden that One placed Cherubim and a flaming sword which turned around to guard the way to the Tree of Life.

1. Using Semitic Parallelism principles, divide the above text into parts (columns) and stanzas.

2. Tape the parts (columns) of stanzas beside each other on the typing paper. Place the stanzas in parallel rows

3. After you have done that, compare your organizational findings with mine below:

Scene 7, Part 1 Gen 3:22a	Scene 7, Part 2 Gen 3:22b	Scene 7, Part 3 Gen 2:23	Scene 7, Part 4 Gen 3:24
Stanza 1	**Stanza 1**	**Stanza 1**	**Stanza 1**
Being-Gods said: "Behold	Now lest he send out his hand to take also of the Tree of Life	Being-Gods sent him out of the Garden of Eden	So Being-Gods drove the man out
Stanza 2	**Stanza 2**	**Stanza 2**	**Stanza 2**
The man has become one of us."	And eat	So that he till the land	And at the east of the Garden of Eden that One placed Cherubim and a flaming sword
Stanza 3	**Stanza 3**	**Stanza 3**	**Stanza 3**
Because he knows good and bad."	And live forever,	From which he was taken.	Which turned around to guard the way to the Tree of Life.

The Structure of the Garden of Eden Allegory			Parallelism Justification
	Scene 4 Gen 3:1-7		**The Keystone Decision:** The man and the woman obtained free choice and used it to put on garments. That led to their punishment and eviction from the Garden that is described in Scenes 5-7.
Scene 3 Gen 2:18-25	→←	**Scene 5** Gen 3:8-13	**An Oppositional Parallel Relationship:** Being-Gods created a woman to help the man in Scene 3. In Scene 5, the man betrays the woman when he blames her for causing him to violate Being-Gods command.
Scene 2 Gen 2:16-17	→←	**Scene 6** Gen 3:14-19	**An Oppositional Parallel Relationship:** Being-Gods issued a command to the Person in Scene 2, and because it was not observed, the person was punished in Scene 6.
Scene 1 Gen 2:4b-9; 2:15	→←	**Scene 7** Gen 3:22-24	**An Oppositional Parallel Relationship:** Being-Gods put the person in the Garden in Scene 1 and drove the person out in Scene 7.

Postscript

The Garden Allegory ends with Gen 3:24. Gen 4:1-25 is an allegory about Cain and Able. The structure of the Cain and Able Allegory does not relate to the structure of the Garden Allegory. Further, the metaphors and other language elements are different in the two allegories. For example, in the Cain and Able Allegory, God is referred to as Being, not Being-Gods. That evidences that the Cain and able allegory was composed later by another author.

Chapter Eleven

A Scene from the Gospel of Luke

Introduction

Luke used Semitic Parallelism to structure his Gospel and convey his meanings. To demonstrate that, we will consider Luke 5:1-10.

Exercise

Copy the text below and on the next page:

Luke 15:1-10

> 15:1 Tax collectors and sinners were drawing near to him to listen to him. 2 And the Pharisees and the Scribes muttered saying: "This one receives sinners to himself and eats with them." 3 Indeed he said to them this parable saying: 4 "What man among you is having one hundred sheep and having lost one of them does not leave the ninety-nine in the wilderness and goes after the one having been lost until he finds it? 5 And having found it, he puts it upon his shoulders rejoicing. 6 And having come into the house he calls together his friends and his neighbors saying to them: 'Rejoice with me because I found my sheep, the one having been lost.'" 7 I say to you:

"In the same way, there will be such joy in heaven over one sinner who repents than upon ninety-nine righteous who do not need repentance. 8 Or what woman having ten drachmas having lost one drachma does not light a lamp and sweep the house seeking carefully until the time when she finds it? 9 And after she found it, she calls together her friends and neighbors saying: 'Rejoice with me because I found the drachma, the one having been lost.' 10 Thus, I say to you: "In the same way, joy comes in the sight of the angels of God over one sinner who repents."

1. Using Semitic Parallelism principles, divide the above text into parts (columns) and stanzas.

2. Tape the parts (columns) of stanzas beside each other on the typing paper. Place the stanzas in parallel rows

3. After you have done that, compare your organizational findings with mine below:

A Scene from the Gospel of Luke

Scene, Intro Lk 5:1-2	Scene, Part 1 Lk 5:3-4	Scene, Part 2 Lk 5:5-6	Scene, Part 3 Lk 5:7
Stanza 1	**Stanza 1**	**Stanza 1**	**Stanza 1**
Tax collectors and sinners were drawing near to him to listen to him	Indeed he said to them this parable saying: "What man among you having one hundred sheep and having lost one of them does not leave the ninety-nine in the wilderness	And having found it he puts it upon his shoulders rejoicing	I say to you: "In the same way there will be such joy in heaven over one sinner
Stanza 2	**Stanza 2**	**Stanza 2**	**Stanza 2**
And the Pharisees and the Scribes muttered saying: "This one receives sinners to himself	And goes after the one having been lost	And having come into the house he calls together his friends and his neighbors saying to them: 'Rejoice with me	Who repents
Stanza 3	**Stanza 3**	**Stanza 3**	**Stanza 3**
And eats with them."	Until he finds it?	Because I found my sheep the one having been lost.'"	Than upon ninety-nine righteous who have no need of repentance.

Scene, Part 1 Lk 5:8	Scene, Part 2 Lk 5:9	Scene, Part 3 Lk 5:10
Stanza 1	**Stanza 1**	**Stanza 1**
Or what woman having ten drachmas having lost one drachma does not light a lamp	And after she found it	Thus, I say to you: "In the same way joy comes in the sight of the angels of God over one sinner
Stanza 2	**Stanza 2**	**Stanza 2**
And sweep the house seeking carefully	She calls together her friends and neighbors saying: 'Rejoice with me	Who repents
Stanza 3	**Stanza 3**	**Stanza 3**
Until the time when she finds it?	Because I found the drachma the one having been lost.	Than upon the many who have no need of repentance."

Chapter Twelve

A Scene from the Gospel of Matthew

Introduction

The Gospel of Matthew is known for Jesus' sermon on the mountain where he preached the Beatitudes. This chapter will demonstrate that Matthew employed Semitic Parallelism to structure that text.

Exercise

Copy the text below and on the next page:

Matthew: 5:1-12

5:1 Indeed, having seen the crowds he went up into the mountain, and having sat down, his disciples came to him, 2 and having opened his mouth, he taught them saying: 3 Blessed are [they who are] 1 poor in spirit for theirs is the kingdom of heaven. 4 Blessed are they who mourn, for they will be comforted. 5 Blessed are [they who are] gentle, for they will inherit the earth. 6 Blessed are they who are hungry and thirsting for righteousness, for they will be satisfied. 7 Blessed are [they who are][31] merciful, for they will obtain mercy. 8 Blessed are [they who are] pure of heart, for they will see God. 9 Blessed are [they who are] peacemakers, for they will be called sons of God. 10 Blessed are they who have been persecuted on account of righteousness, for theirs is the kingdom of heaven. 11 Blessed are you when people revile you and persecute you and say all manner of evil against you falsely on account of me; 12 rejoice and exult, for great is your reward in heaven, for in this manner they persecuted the prophets before you."

1. Using Semitic Parallelism principles, divide the above text into parts (columns) and stanzas.

2. Tape the parts (columns) of stanzas beside each other on the typing paper. Place the stanzas in parallel rows

3. After you have done that, compare your organizational findings with mine below:

---

[31] *Brackets:* Text that a scribe deleted from the original.

A Scene from the Gospel of Matthew

Scene, Intro. Mt 5:1-2	Scene, Part 1, Mt 5:3	Scene, Part 2, Mt 5:4	Scene, Part 3, Mt 5:5	Scene, Part 4, Mt 5:6
Stanza 1	**Stanza 1**	**Stanza 1**	**Stanza 1**	**Stanza 1**
Indeed, having seen the crowds he went up into the mountain	Blessed are [they	Blessed are they	Blessed are [they	Blessed are they
Stanza 2	**Stanza 2**	**Stanza 2**	**Stanza 2**	**Stanza 2**
And having sat down his disciples came to him	Who are] poor in spirit	Who mourn	Who are] gentle	Who are hungry and thirsting for righteousness
Stanza 3	**Stanza 3**	**Stanza 3**	**Stanza 3**	**Stanza 3**
And having opened his mouth he taught them saying:	For theirs is the kingdom of heaven.	For they will be comforted.	For they will inherit the earth.	For they will be satisfied.

Scene, Part 5, Mt 5:7	Scene, Part 6, Mt 5:8	Scene, Part 7, Mt 5:9	Scene, Part 8, Mt 5:10
Stanza 1	**Stanza 1**	**Stanza 1**	**Stanza 1**
Blessed are [they	Blessed are [they	Blessed are [they	Blessed are they
Stanza 2	**Stanza 2**	**Stanza 2**	**Stanza 2**
Who are] merciful	Who are] pure of heart	Who are] peacemakers	Who have been persecuted on account of righteousness
Stanza 3	**Stanza 3**	**Stanza 3**	**Stanza 3**
For they will obtain mercy.	For they will see God.	For they will be called sons of God.	For theirs is the kingdom of heaven.[40]

[32] Verses 11 and 12 were inserted by a scribe after the original was completed. We know that because:

1. Verses 11 and 12 cannot be divided into columns with three stanzas in each column.

2. The language structure of verses 11 and 12 differs greatly from the previous verses.

3. The tone of verses 11 and 12 changes from a formal statement to an exhortation to people being persecuted. Therefore, it is likely that someone in authority, such as a Christian Bishop, ordered a scribe to insert these words to encourage his subjects who were suffering.

4. Verses 11 and 12 unnecessarily repeat what has been said succinctly in Part 8.

5. Verses 11 and 12 do not parallel Part 1, which they should do if they ended it. Part 8, does parallel Part 1. Notice especially the third Stanzas.

Chapter Thirteen

A Scene from the Gospel of John

Introduction

John also used SP to arrange his Gospel and disclose his meanings. We will consider 2:1-10 to show that.

Exercise

Copy the text below:

John 2:1-10

2:1 On the third day, there was a wedding in Cana of Galilee, and the mother of Jesus was there, 2 and both Jesus and his disciples were invited to the wedding. 3 When the wine ran out the mother of Jesus said to him: "They have no wine." 4 And Jesus said to her: "So [what are you asking]? My hour has not yet come." 5 His mother said to the servants: "Whatever he says to you, do it." 6 Now six stone water jars were sitting there for the Jewish purification containing 20 or 30 measures each. 7 Jesus said to them: "Fill the jars with water." So they filled them up to the brim. 8 And he said to them: "Draw some out now and take it to the headwaiter." So they took it. 9 When the headwaiter tasted the water having become wine, he did not know from where it had come; but the servants who had drawn the water, they knew [from where it had come.][33] So the headwaiter called the bridegroom and said to him: 10 "Every man serves the good wine first and after much drinking, he serves the lesser wine. This is the beginning of the signs that Jesus did in Cana of Galilee. And his disciples believed in him.

1. Using Semitic Parallelism principles, divide the above text into an introduction, scenes, and parts.

2. Tape the columns of stanzas beside each other on the typing paper. Place the stanzas in parallel rows

3. After you have done that, compare your organizational findings with mine below:

---

[33] *Brackets:* Text deleted by a scribe.

A Scene from the Gospel of John

Scene Part 1 John 2:1-2	Scene Part 2 John 2:3	Scene Part 3 John 2:4	Scene Part 4 John 2:5	Scene Part 5 John 2:6
Stanza 1	**Stanza 1**	**Stanza 1**	**Stanza 1**	**Stanza 1**
On the third day there was a wedding in Cana of Galilee	When the wine ran out the mother of Jesus said to him: "They have no wine."	His mother said to the servants: "Whatever [it is	Now six stone water jars were sitting there for the Jewish purification containing 20 or 30 measures each.	And he said to them: "Draw some out now
Stanza 2	**Stanza 2**	**Stanza 2**	**Stanza 2**	**Stanza 2**
And the mother of Jesus was there	And Jesus said to her: "So [what are you asking]?	That] he says to you	Jesus said to them: "Fill the jars with water."	And take it to the headwaiter."
Stanza 3	**Stanza 3**	**Stanza 3**	**Stanza 3**	**Stanza 3**
And both Jesus and his disciples were invited to the wedding.	My hour has not yet come."	Do it."	So they filled them up to the brim.	So they took it.

Scene Part 6 John 2:7	Scene Part 7 John 2:8	Scene Part 8 John 2:9	Scene Part 9 John 2:10
Stanza 1	**Stanza 1**	**Stanza 1**	**Stanza 1**
When the headwaiter tasted the water having become wine	But the servants who had drawn the water,	So the headwaiter called the bridegroom	This is the beginning of the signs
Stanza 2	**Stanza 2**	**Stanza 2**	**Stanza 2**
He did not know from where	They knew [from where.	And said to him: "Every man serves the good wine first	That Jesus did in Cana of Galilee
Stanza 3	**Stanza 3**	**Stanza 3**	**Stanza 3**
It had come;	It had come.]	And after much drinking he serves the lesser wine.	And his disciples believed in him.

Chapter Fourteen
The Covenant

Introduction

Over 2500 years ago, an unknown author wrote about a man named Abraham, and how God gave him a Covenant that has since shaped the lives of billions of Jews, Christians, and Muslims. We will now use the Semitic Parallelism principles to examine the structure of the Covenant.

Exercise

Copy the text below and on the next page.

Genesis 12:1-3

12:1 Yĕhovah (Being) said to Abraham: "Go from the land of your tribes and of your father's house to the earth[34] that I will show you, 2 and I will make a great nation [of you].[35] And I will bless you, and [I] will magnify your name greatly, and you will be a blessing to others. 3 And I will bless them, [The ones who magnify your name] and who bless you, and I will curse them, [the ones who do not magnify your name], and who

---

[34] The Hebrew word here is "'erets," which most translate as "land." We will see below, that the structure of this text shows that the original was probably the Hebrew word," 'adamah," which I translate as "earth." See our discussion of Gen 2:4b-15 above.

[35] Text in brackets is required by the structure. A scribe omitted it.

> curse you. And all tribes will be blessed in the earth [that I will show you, the ones who are a great nation].

1. Using Semitic Parallelism principles, divide the above text into parts and stanzas.

2. Tape the columns of stanzas beside each other on the typing paper. Place the stanzas in parallel rows.

3. Then, in another layout, place each **Part** in an arch.

4. After you have done that, compare your organizational findings with mine below.

Part 1 Gen 12:1-2a	Part 2 Gen 12: 2b	Part 3 Gen 12:3a	Part 4 Gen 12:3b	Part 5 Gen 12:3c
Stanza 1	**Stanza 1**	**Stanza 1**	**Stanza 1**	**Stanza 1**
Being said to Abraham: Go from the land of your tribes and of your father's house to the earth	And I will bless you	And I will bless them	And I will curse them	And all tribes will be blessed in the earth
Stanza 2	**Stanza 2**	**Stanza 2**	**Stanza 2**	**Stanza 2**
That I will show you	And [I] will magnify your name greatly	[The ones who magnify your name]	[The ones who do not magnify your name]	[That I will show you],
Stanza 3	**Stanza 3**	**Stanza 3**	**Stanza 3**	**Stanza 3**
And I will make a great nation [of you].	And you will be a blessing.	And who bless you;	And who curse you.	[The ones who are a great nation].

As you can see above, the structure demands the words like those in brackets. They were left out of our current Hebrew text by copyists over the centuries.

The author also structured the Covenant in an arch as we see below:

	Part 3, Gen 12:3a	
	Stanza 1 And I will bless them	
Part 2, Gen 12: 2b	**Stanza 2** [The ones who magnify your name]	**Part 4, Gen 12:3b**
Stanza 1 And I will bless you	**Stanza 3** And who bless you;	**Stanza 1** And I will curse them
Stanza 2 And [I] will magnify your name greatly	→↑← Oppositional Parallel Relationship	**Stanza 2** [The ones who do not magnify your name]
Stanza 3 And you will be a blessing.		**Stanza 3** And who curse you.
Part 1, Gen 12:1-2a		**Part 5, Gen 12:3c**
Stanza 1 Being said to Abraham: Go from the land of your tribes and of your father's house to the earth		**Stanza 1** And all tribes will be blessed in the earth
Stanza 2 That I will show you	←↑→ The Equivalent Parallel Relationship	**Stanza 2** [That I will show you],
Stanza 3 And I will make a great nation [of you].		**Stanza 3** [The ones who are a great nation].

In my book, *The Second Coming of Eve, Abraham, Buddha, and Jesus*, I argue that 'erets should be translated as "land," and 'adama as "earth." Copyists of early manuscripts sometimes substituted 'erets for 'adama, and vice versa.

Most translations of Part 1, Stanzas 1-2 read: "Go from the land of your tribe and of your father's house to the "land" ('erets) that I will show you." I translate the last part of that sentence "to the earth that I will show you." I do that because we can see that the parallel Stanza 1 in Part 4 uses for the word "earth" ('adama). That is the first clue that a copyist changed 'erets to adama.

We also have another reason to think that a copyist made that change. In our discussion of Gen 2:4b-15, I argued that 'erets is a metaphor for unconsciousness or semi-consciousness, and that 'adama is a metaphor for reflective consciousness. As we grow, we reflect on our unconscious and semi-conscious thoughts in order to make them conscious and available for personal development. So, the meaning of the Covenant command is this: "Go from the unconscious beliefs (land) of your family and father to the conscious life (earth) to which I, Being will lead you.

Chapter Fifteen

A Scene from the Gospel of Thomas

Exercise 21

Please copy the following text.

Gospel of Thomas
Saying 7

A blest one, he is the lion; the one that the man will eat and the lion comes to be the man. And he is cursed, namely the man, the one that the lion will eat and the lion comes to be the man.

1. `Using Semitic Parallelism principles, divide the above text into parts and stanzas. **Note:** In *The Gospel of Thomas*, we often find more than three stanzas in a Part (column).

2. Tape the columns of stanzas beside each other on the typing paper. Place the stanzas in parallel rows.

3. Then, in another layout, place each part in an arch.

4. After you have done that, compare your organizational findings with mine below.

Saying 7, Part 1	Saying 7, Part 2
Stanza 1 A blest one[45]	**Stanza 1** And he is cursed
Stanza 1 He is the lion	**Stanza 1** Namely the man[32]
Stanza 1 The one[32]	**Stanza 1** The one[32]
Stanza 1 That the man will eat	**Stanza 1** That the lion will eat
Stanza 1 And the lion comes to be the man.	**Stanza 1** And the lion comes to be the man.

---

[36] The verb in the Stanza is implied.

	Saying 7 Part 1				**Saying 7 Part 2**	
	The one				The one	
He is the lion	←↑→	That the man will eat	→← Oppositional Parallel Relationship	Namely the man	←↑→	That the lion will eat
A blest one	←↑→	And the lion comes to be the man.		And he is cursed	←↑→	And the lion comes to be the man.

This is a very clever two-part poem. Jesus, the author, organized it in parallel columns and in an arch.

In this Poem, the "lion" is a person like Abraham who has left the expectations of his society and his family to listen to Spirit. As a result, he speaks the words of Spirit to the "man" who "eats" (listens). As a result, that "man" is "blessed" by becoming in spirit like the lion.

In contrast, a "man" who does not listen to a lion-person like Abraham becomes "cursed." The lion-person sees through him and makes life difficult for him.

Chapter Sixteen
Final Comments

This Workbook has shown that some Biblical authors employed Semitic Parallelism both to structure their works and to convey the meaning of metaphors, sections, and the entire text. This method also enabled them to help their future audience detect later scribal errors and edits. One might wonder, therefore, if all of the Biblical authors used Semitic Parallelism, and if that method was also used in other Semitic texts, and even, in ancient non-Semitic literature. I can partially answer those questions from my limited research.

I investigated small sections of many texts in the Old Testament. I found that the authors of the Pentateuch in general employed Semitic Parallelism. However, parts of those books do not. For example, The authors of the sections narrating genealogies and the Torah Laws did not use Semitic Parallelism to structure the text. That is evidence that these texts were later insertions by other authors.

As for the rest of the Old Testament, some authors used Semitic Parallelism; others did not. And again, I found that in works where the authors employed the ancient methodology, there are clear insertions by authors that do not use it.

In the New Testament, Matthew, Mark, Luke, and John used SP. The letters of Paul, James, and Peter, and the Acts of the Apostles do not seem to possess a SP structure. I was able to apply SP successfully to some parts of the Book of Revelations and not to other parts. The same is true for the letters of John.

Concerning other Semitic texts, I used Semitic Parallelism to discern the organization and meaning of *The Gospel of Thomas*. That discovery indicates that the ancient methodology was used by Semitic authors whose works were not included in the Bible.

Additional Reading

For a further detailed explanation of Semitic Parallelism, see the extensive Appendices in my book: *The Gospel of Thomas in its Original Poetic Arrangement—Professional Edition*. At the end of the Book, I present 14 arguments that Jesus was the probable author.

The Gospel of Thomas lays out a full theory of personal development that could be taught in any psychology curriculum. Because of my Ph.D. degree in Counseling, I was able to discern Jesus' therapeutic methods and arrange his wisdom poems to explain them. That information is in the book: *The Messiah's Unrealized Revolution Discovered in the Gospel of Thomas*. In that book I also contrasted Jesus' philosophy of personal growth with that of Paul the Apostle and most Christian clergy today.

In my book, *The Second Coming of Eve, Abraham, Buddha, and Jesus—Their soul Way to Personal and Global Peace,* I demonstrate how to identify and read ancient allegories. I also explain the meaning of the wisdom metaphors that were used throughout the Middle East before the Second Century CE.

We send out periodic emails about new publications by me and others. You can register at www.7771.org to receive them.

Appendix

Act One of the Gospel of Mark

To better conceptualize and analyze Act 1 of Mark, we suggest that you copy or print Act 1. It is below. Then, clip the pages together. In that way, you can remove pages and study them side by side.

Notice:

- In the Act 1 text below, the notes are END NOTES. You will find them on the last page.

- Scenes 7-12 were put out of order by a copyist. I put them back in order. They now parallel each other correctly.

The Organization of the Gospel of Mark and Act One: 1:1-3:34

The Organization of the Gospel of Mark

	Act 7 Mk 11:1-33	
Act 6 Mk 8:22-26,[1] 10:13-50	↓↑	**Act 8** Mk 12:1-44
Act 5 Mk 8:27-9:42	↓↑	**Act 9** Mk 13:1-37
Act 4 Mk 6:14-8:21	↓↑	**Act 10** Mk 14:1-26
Act 3 Mk 4:35-6:1	↓↑	**Act 11** Mk 14:27-72
Act 2 Mk 4:1-34	↓↑	**Act 12** Mk 15:1-39
Act 1 Mk 1:1-3:34	↓↑	**Act 13** Mk 15:40-16:1-8

The Organization of Act One: 1:1-3:34

Scene 9 Mk 2:1-12b	↓↑	**Scene 10** Mk 2:13-17
Scene 8 Mk 2:18-22	↓↑	**Scene 11** Mk 2:23-28
Scene 7 Mk 1:35-39	↓↑	**Scene 12** Mk 1:40-45b
Scene 6 Mk 1:29-34b	↓↑	**Scene 13** Mk 3:1-6
Scene 5 Mk 1:21-28	↓↑	**Scene 14** Mk 3:7-12
Scene 4 Mk 1:16-20	↓↑	**Scene 15** Mk 3:13-19a
Scene 3 Mk 1:14-15	↓↑	**Scene 16** Mk 3:19b-21
Scene 2 Mk 1:9-13	↓↑	**Scene 17** Mk 3:22-29
Scene 1 Mk 1:1-8	↓↑↓	**Scene 18** Mk 3:31-34

Appendix Act One of the Gospel of Mark

Act 1, Scene 1, Part 1 Mk 1:2	Act 1, Scene 1, Part 2 Mk 1:3	Act 1, Scene 1, Part 3 Mk 1:4	Act 1, Scene 1, Part 4 Mk 1:5	Act 1, Scene 1, Part 5 Mk 1:6-7
Stanza 1 ²As it has been written in Isaiah the prophet: "Behold	**Stanza 1** A voice crying out in the wilderness	**Stanza 1** John came baptizing in the wilderness	**Stanza 1** And all the Judean countryside and all of the Jerusalemites were going out to him	**Stanza 1** And John was clothed with the hairs of a camel with a leather girdle about his loins and eating locusts and wild honey
Stanza 2 I send my messenger before your face	**Stanza 2** 'Make ready the way of the Lord	**Stanza 2** And he was preaching a baptism of repentance	**Stanza 2** And they were baptized by him in the Jordan River	**Stanza 2** He was preaching saying: "The one stronger than me after me comes
Stanza 3 Who will prepare your way before you;	**Stanza 3** Make straight his paths.'"	**Stanza 3** In order that one be released³ of his sins.	**Stanza 3** And they openly confessed their sins	**Stanza 3** Of whom not I am sufficient having stooped to loosen the laces of his sandals;

Act 1, Scene 1, Part 6 Mk 1:8
Stanza 1
[Behold him,]
Stanza 2
I baptized you with water
Stanza 3
But he will baptize you with the Holy Spirit."

Appendix Act One of the Gospel of Mark

Act 1, Scene 2, Part 1 Mk 1:9-10	Act 1, Scene 2, Part 2 Mk 1:11-12	Act 1, Scene 2, Part 3 Mk 1:13
Stanza 1 And it occurred in those days that Jesus came from Nazareth of Galilee	**Stanza 1** And a voice occurred out of the heavens saying: "You are my son the loved	**Stanza 1** And he was in the wilderness for 40 days being tempted by Satan
Stanza 2 And he was baptized in the Jordan by John.	**Stanza 2** In you I am well pleased."	**Stanza 2** And he was with the wild beasts
Stanza 3 And immediately going up out of the water he saw the heavens split and the spirit as a dove coming down on him.	**Stanza 3** And immediately his spirit thrust him out into the wilderness.	**Stanza 3** And the angels were serving him.

Act 1, Scene 3, Part 1 Mk 1:14		Act 1, Scene 3, Part 2 Mk 1:15	
Stanza 1		Stanza 1	
And after the delivering up of John Jesus came into Galilee		And has drawn near the Kingdom of God.	
Stanza 2		Stanza 2	
And he preached the gospel of God		Repent	
Stanza 3		Stanza 3	
Saying: "The appointed time has been fulfilled		And believe in the gospel."	

Appendix Act One of the Gospel of Mark

Act 1, Scene 4, Part 1 Mk 1:16-18	Act 1, Scene 4, Part 2 Mk 1:19-20
Stanza 1	**Stanza 1**
And passing by the sea of Galilee he saw Simon and Andrew the brother of Simon casting their nets into the sea[4]	And stepping on a little he saw James the son of Zebedee and John his brother in the boat mending their nets
Stanza 2	**Stanza 2**
And he said to them: "Here behind me."[5]	And immediately he called them
Stanza 3	**Stanza 3**
And immediately having released the nets they followed him.	And after releasing their father Zebedee in the boat with the hired men they went off behind him.

Act 1, Scene 5, Part 1 Mk 1:21-22	Act 1, Scene 5, Part 2 Mk 1:23-24	Act 1, Scene 5, Part 3 Mk 1:25-26	Act 1, Scene 5, Part 4 Mk 1:27a	Act 1, Scene 5, Part 5 Mk 1:27b-28
Stanza 1	Stanza 1	Stanza 1	Stanza 1	Stanza 1
And having entered Capernaum and immediately on the Sabbath in the synagogue he was teaching	And immediately a man with an unclean spirit was in their synagogue crying out: "Do you want to destroy us Jesus of Nazareth?	And Jesus having rebuked it said: Be muzzled	And all were astonished so as to be gathering together	[For when he rebukes them]
Stanza 2	Stanza 2	Stanza 2	Stanza 2	Stanza 2
And they were astounded by his teaching	I understand who you are.	And come forth out of him.	Saying: "What is this a new teaching?	They obey him."
Stanza 3	Stanza 3	Stanza 3	Stanza 3	Stanza 3
For he was teaching them with authority and not as the Scribes.	You are the holy one of God.	And the unclean spirit having convulsed him and having yelled with a great voice came forth out of him.	With authority he gives orders to the unclean spirits	Therefore went forth his reputation immediately everywhere in the whole country around Galilee.

Appendix Act One of the Gospel of Mark

Act 1, Scene 6, Part 1 Mk 1:29-30	Act 1, Scene 6, Part 2 Mk:1 31-32	Act 1, Scene 6, Part 3 Mk 1:32	Act 1, Scene 6, Part 4 Mk 1:33-34a	Act 1, Scene 6, Part 5 Mk 1:34b
Stanza 1	Stanza 1	Stanza 1	Stanza 1	Stanza 1
And immediately having gone forth out of the synagogue they came into the house of Simon and Andrew with James and John.	And having come to her he raised her up having taken hold of her hand	Indeed evening having occurred when the sun set	And the whole city was gathered at the door	[And because the whole city was gathered at the door]
Stanza 2	Stanza 2	Stanza 2	Stanza 2	Stanza 2
Indeed the mother-in-law of Simon was lying down burning with fever	And the fever released her	They we're bringing to him all the ill	And he cured many ill to various sicknesses	He did not release the demons to be speaking
Stanza 3	Stanza 3	Stanza 3	Stanza 3	Stanza 3
So immediately they chattered with him about her.	And she was serving them.	And those demonized	And he threw out many demons,	Because they understood him to be Christ.

Act 1, Scene 7, Part 1 Mk 1:35	Act 1, Scene 7, Part 2 Mk 1:36-37	Act 1, Scene 7, Part 3 Mk 1:38	Act 1, Scene 7, Part 4 Mk 1:39
Stanza 1	Stanza 1	Stanza 1	Stanza 1
And early in the morning very much in the night having stood up he went out	And Simon and the ones with him pursued him	And he said to them: "Let us go elsewhere into the near cities	For this I went out."
Stanza 2	Stanza 2	Stanza 2	Stanza 2
And he went off into the wilderness place	And they found him	In order that also there I might preach	And he came preaching into their synagogues in the whole of Galilee
Stanza 3	Stanza 3	Stanza 3	Stanza 3
And there he was praying.	And they chattered to him: "All are seeking you."	[And throw out demons	And he threw out the demons.]

Act 1, Scene 8, Part 1　Mk 2:18	Act 1, Scene 8, Part 2　Mk 2:19	Act 1, Scene 8, Part 3　Mk 2:20	Act 1, Scene 8, Part 4　Mk 2:21	Act 1, Scene 8, Part 5　Mk 2:22
Stanza 1	Stanza 1	Stanza 1	Stanza 1	Stanza 1
The disciples of John and the Pharisees were fasting.	And Jesus said to them: "The sons of the bride chamber	Indeed days will come	Nobody sews a patch of unshrunk cloth upon an old outer garment	And nobody thrusts new wine into old skin bags
Stanza 2	Stanza 2	Stanza 2	Stanza 2	Stanza 2
And people having come said: "Why are the disciples of John and the Pharisees fasting	When the bridegroom is with them	When the bridegroom will be released from them	Because indeed the fullness of the new one raises it up from the old one	Because indeed the wine will burst the skin bags losing the wine and the skin bags.
Stanza 3	Stanza 3	Stanza 3	Stanza 3	Stanza 3
But your disciples are not fasting?"	They are not able to fast.	And then they will fast on that day.	And it becomes a worse split.	But one thrusts new wine into new skin bags."

Act 1, Scene 9, Part 1 Mk 2:1	Act 1, Scene 9, Part 2 Mk 2:2	Act 1, Scene 9, Part 3 Mk 2:3-4a	Act 1, Scene 9, Part 4 Mk 2:6-7	Act 1, Scene 9, Part 5 Mk 2:8
Stanza 1	Stanza 1	Stanza 1	Stanza 1	Stanza 1
And after some days having entered into Capernaum it was heard	And he was speaking to them the word.	Where Jesus was.	Indeed some of the Scribes were sitting there reasoning in their hearts:	And immediately Jesus having recognized in his spirit that thus they are reasoning in themselves
Stanza 2	Stanza 2	Stanza 2	Stanza 2	Stanza 2
That he is in a house	And they came bringing to him a paralytic being raised up by four	And having dug out the roof they lowered the cot with the paralytic lying on it.	"Why does this one blaspheme	Said to them: "Why are you reasoning like this?
Stanza 3	Stanza 3	Stanza 3	Stanza 3	Stanza 3
And so many having gathered that indeed there was no room, not even places near the door.	And not being able to bring him near to Jesus because of the crowd they removed the roof	And Jesus having seen their faith said to the paralytic: "Child your sins are released."	Who is able to release sins except the one God?"	Which is easier to say to the paralytic 'Your sins are released'

Act 1, Scene 9, Part 6 Mk 2:9b	Act 1, Scene 9, Part 7 Mk 2:10-11	Act 1, Scene 9, Part 8 Mk 2:12a	Act 1, Scene 9, Part 9 Mk 2:12b
Stanza 1	**Stanza 1**	**Stanza 1**	**Stanza 1**
Or to say: 'Get up	⁶"Therefore to you I say: "Get up!	And he got up	So that they were outside of themselves
Stanza 2	**Stanza 2**	**Stanza 2**	**Stanza 2**
Raise up your cot	'Raise up your cot	And immediately raised up his cot	And they glorified God
Stanza 3	**Stanza 3**	**Stanza 3**	**Stanza 3**
And walk about?'	And go to your house.'"	And went out in front of all	Saying: "We never saw anything like this."

Act 1, Scene 10, Part 1 Mk 2:13	Act 1, Scene 10, Part 2 Mk 2:14	Act 1, Scene 10, Part 13 Mk 2:15	Act 1, Scene 10, Part 4 Mk 2:16	Act 1, Scene 10, Part 5 Mk 2:17
Stanza 1	Stanza 1	Stanza 1	Stanza 1	Stanza 1
And he went out again beside the sea	And passing by he saw Levi the son of Alphaeus sitting upon the tax office	And it occurs that he was reclining at table in Levi's house	And the Scribes of the Pharisees saw	And Jesus having heard said to them: "The strong do not have a need of a healer
Stanza 2	Stanza 2	Stanza 2	Stanza 2	Stanza 2
And all the crowd was coming to him	And he said to him: "Be following me."	And many tax collectors and sinners were reclining with Jesus and his disciples	That he eats with the sinners and tax collectors	But the ones who are ill;
Stanza 3	Stanza 3	Stanza 3	Stanza 3	Stanza 3
And he was teaching them.	And having stood up he followed him.	For many were following him.	And they chattered to his disciples: "He eats with the tax collectors and sinners."	I came not to call the righteous but sinners."

Act 1, Scene 11, Part 1 Mk 2:23	Act 1, Scene 11, Part 2 Mk 2:24	Act 1, Scene 11, Part 3 Mk 2:25	Act 1, Scene 11, Part 4 Mk 2:26	Act 1, Scene 11, Part 5 Mk 2:27-28
Stanza 1 And it happened that he proceeded through the grain fields on the Sabbath	**Stanza 1** And the Pharisees chattered to him: "Notice	**Stanza 1** And he said to them: "Never did you read	**Stanza 1** How he having entered the house of God with Abiathar as chief priest and ate the loaves of bread of the presentation	**Stanza 1** And he said to them: "The Sabbath came to be because of man
Stanza 2 And his disciples began to make their way	**Stanza 2** Why are they doing on the Sabbath	**Stanza 2** What David did when in need	**Stanza 2** Which it is not lawful to eat except by the priests	**Stanza 2** And not the man came to be because of the Sabbath
Stanza 3 While they plucked the heads of grain.	**Stanza 3** What is not lawful?"	**Stanza 3** When he and the ones with him got hungry?	**Stanza 3** And also he gave some to the ones with him?"	**Stanza 3** Thus the son of man is lord also of the Sabbath."

Act 1, Scene 12, Part 1 Mk 1:40	Act 1, Scene 12, Part 2 Mk 1:41	Act 1, Scene 12, Part 3 Mk 1:42	Act 1, Scene 12, Part 4 Mk 1:43-44a	Act 1, Scene 12, Part 5 Mk 1:44b
Stanza 1	Stanza 1	Stanza 1	Stanza 1	Stanza 1
And a leper came toward him entreating him	And having been moved with pity and having stretched out his hand he touched him	And immediately the leprosy went off from him	And having given strict orders to him immediately he thrust him out	But go
Stanza 2	Stanza 2	Stanza 2	Stanza 2	Stanza 2
And kneeling down said to him: "If you will it	And said to him: "I am willing	[Because Jesus willed it][7]	And said to him: "See	Show yourself to the Priest
Stanza 3	Stanza 3	Stanza 3	Stanza 3	Stanza 3
You are able to make me clean."	Be cleansed."	And he was cleansed.	That you tell nothing to anyone	And bring the things directed by Moses as a witness to them regarding your cleansing."

Act 1, Scene 12, Part 6 Mk 1:45a	Act 1, Scene 12, Part 7 Mk 1:45b
Stanza 1	**Stanza 1**
The leper indeed having gone out began to proclaim many things	Therefore he was out in wilderness places
Stanza 2	**Stanza 2**
And to spread abroad the word	[And he was teaching them]
Stanza 3	**Stanza 3**
So that he was not able manifestly to enter a city.	And they were coming to him from all sides.

Act 1, Scene 13, Part 1 Mk 3:1	Act 1, Scene 13, Part 2 Mk 3:2	Act 1, Scene 13, Part 3 Mk 3:3-4	Act 1, Scene 13, Part 4 Mk 3:5	Act 1, Scene 13, Part 5 Mk 3:6
Stanza 1	**Stanza 1**	**Stanza 1**	**Stanza 1**	**Stanza 1**
And again he entered a synagogue	And they were observing him	And he said to the man to the one with the withered hand: "Get up in the midst of everyone."	And having looked around on them with wrath being thoroughly grieved by their dull hearts he said to the man: "Stretch out your hand."	And having gone out immediately the Pharisees with the Herodians gathered to take counsel
Stanza 2	**Stanza 2**	**Stanza 2**	**Stanza 2**	**Stanza 2**
And a man was there	To determine whether he would cure him on the Sabbath	And he said to them "Is it lawful on the Sabbath to do good or to do bad, to save a soul or to kill one?"	And he stretched out his hand	And they condemned him
Stanza 3	**Stanza 3**	**Stanza 3**	**Stanza 3**	**Stanza 3**
And he had a dried up hand.	In order that they might accuse him.	Indeed they were silent.	And it was restored.	In order that they might destroy him.

Appendix Act One of the Gospel of Mark

Act 1, Scene 14, Part 1 Mk 3:7-8	Act 1, Scene 14, Part 2 Mk 3:9	Act 1, Scene 14, Part 3 Mk 3:10	Act 1, Scene 14, Part 4 Mk 3:11	Act 1, Scene 14, Part 5 Mk 3:12
Stanza 1 And Jesus with his disciples withdrew to the sea	**Stanza 1** And he told his disciples	**Stanza 1** For he cured many	**Stanza 1** And the unclean spirits whenever they were beholding him	**Stanza 1** [And because they beheld him]
Stanza 2 And a great multitude from the Galilee and from the Judea and from Jerusalem and from the Idumea and from the other side of the Jordan and from Tyre and Sidon hearing the many things he is doing	**Stanza 2** That a little boat should constantly be serviceable to him	**Stanza 2** With the result that many with scourges were falling upon him	**Stanza 2** They fell down before him	**Stanza 2** He said many things in rebuke of them
Stanza 3 Came to him.	**Stanza 3** In order that the crowd not press upon him.	**Stanza 3** In order that he might touch them.	**Stanza 3** And cried out saying: "You are the son of God."	**Stanza 3** In order that they should not make him manifest.

Act 1, Scene 15, Part 1 Mk 3:13	Act 1, Scene 15, Part 2 Mk 3:14-15	Act 1, Scene 15, Part 3 Mk 3:16-19a
Stanza 1	Stanza 1	Stanza 1
And after stepping up on the mountain he called to himself	And he made a group of twelve	And he made a group of twelve
Stanza 2	Stanza 2	Stanza 2
Whom he wanted	Whom he called "apostles"	And he called Simon[8] and James the son of Zebedee and John, the brother of James[9] and Andrew and Philip and Bartholomew and Matthew and Thomas and James the son of Alphaeus and Thaddaeus and Simon the Cananaean and Judas Iscariot
Stanza 3	Stanza 3	Stanza 3
And they went to him.	In order that they might be with him to be sent off to preach and to throw out demons with authority.	Who also delivered him up.

Act 1, Scene 16, Part 1 Mk 3:19b-20	Act 1, Scene 16, Part 2 Mk 3:21
Stanza 1	**Stanza 1**
And he comes into a house	And his friends heard about him
Stanza 2	**Stanza 2**
And the crowd gathered again	And they went out to lay hold of him
Stanza 3	**Stanza 3**
So that they were not able even to eat bread.	For they were chattering: That he is outside of himself.

Act 1, Scene 17, Part 1 Mk 3:22	Act 1, Scene 17, Part 2 Mk 3:23-24	Act 1, Scene 17, Part 3 Mk 3:25	Act 1, Scene 17, Part 4 Mk 3:26	Act 1, Scene 17, Part 5 Mk 3:27
Stanza 1	**Stanza 1**	**Stanza 1**	**Stanza 1**	**Stanza 1**
And the Scribes the ones from Jerusalem came down	And having called them to himself he said to them in parables: "How is Satan able to throw out Satan?	[And he said to them Again is Satan able to throw out Satan?]	And if Satan should rise up against himself	Rather one is not able to enter the house of the strong one to plunder his vessels
Stanza 2	**Stanza 2**	**Stanza 2**	**Stanza 2**	**Stanza 2**
And they chattered That he has Beelzebul	For if a Kingdom should be divided	For if a house should be divided against itself	And becomes divided	Unless he first binds the strong one
Stanza 3	**Stanza 3**	**Stanza 3**	**Stanza 3**	**Stanza 3**
And that he throws out demons by means of the ruler of the demons.	That Kingdom is not able to stand.	That house will not be able to stand	He is not able to stand.[10]	And then he will plunder his house.

Act 1, Scene 17, Part 6 Mk 3:28-29	Act 1, Scene 17, Part 7 Mk 3:29
Stanza 1	**Stanza 1**
Amen I am saying to you: 'All things the sons of men have done including their sins and blasphemes	But who should blaspheme the Holy Spirit
Stanza 2	**Stanza 2**
Will be released;	He will not be released ever
Stanza 3	**Stanza 3**
However many they might blasphemously commit.	But he is held in an everlasting sin.'[11]

Act 1, Scene 18, Part 1 Mk 3:31-32	Act 1, Scene 18, Part 2 Mk 3:32	Act 1, Scene 18, Part 3 Mk 3:33-34
Stanza 1	Stanza 1	Stanza 1
And his mother and his brothers came	And a crowd was sitting about him	And Jesus answered them by saying: "Who is my mother and my brothers?"
Stanza 2	Stanza 2	Stanza 2
And they stood outside	And they chattered: "Behold you mother and your brothers outside	And having looked around on the ones about him sitting in a circle he said: "Behold my mother and my brothers!
Stanza 3	Stanza 3	Stanza 3
And they sent in to him calling him.	And they are seeking you."	The one having done the will of God is my brother and sister and mother."

Appendix Act One of the Gospel of Mark

Two Parallel Column Organization			Parallelism Justification
Scene 9 Mk 2:1-12b	↔	**Scene 10** Mk 2:13-17	**An Equivalent Relationship:** The theme in Scenes 9 and 10 is the same: "I came not to call the righteous, but sinners."
Scene 8 Mk 2:18-22	↔	**Scene 11** Mk 2:23-28	Scenes 8-11 have an **Equivalent Relationship:** They are united by the theme of hunger and the statement that Jesus is lord over all Torah Laws.
Scene 7 Mk 1:35-39	↔	**Scene 12** Mk 1:40-45b	Scenes 7 and 12 have an **Analogous Relationship.** Driving out demons in 7 is analogous to cleansing in 12. Both actions result in crowds coming to Jesus.
Scene 6 Mk 1:29-34b	↔	**Scene 13** Mk 3:1-6	**An Equivalent Relationships:** Jesus cures in Scenes 6 and 13.
Scene 5 Mk 1:21-28	↔	**Scene 14** Mk 3:7-12	**An Equivalent Relationship:** In Scene 5, people declare Jesus as the "holy one of God." In Scene 14, they declare him as the "son of God." In both scenes, he rebukes the unclean spirits who behold and announce him.
Scene 4 Mk 1:16-20	↔	**Scene 15** Mk 3:13-19a	**A Stage 1-Stage 2 Relationship:** Jesus begins selecting his disciples in Scene 4. He chooses more in Scene 15.
Scene 3 Mk 1:14-15	↔	**Scene 16** Mk 3:19b-21	**An Oppositional Relationship:** Jesus' friends in Scene 16 oppose Jesus because of the message he preaches in Scene 3.
Scene 2 Mk 1:9-13	↔	**Scene 17** Mk 3:22-29	**An Equivalent Relationship:** Scenes 2 and 17 explain the roles of the Holy Spirit and Satan.
Scene 1 Mk 1:1-8	↔	**Scene 18** Mk 3:31-34	**An Equivalent Relationship:** In Scenes 1 John preaches the Torah, and in Scene 18, Jesus mother and brothers live the Torah. **An Oppositional Relationship:** In Scene 1, John endorses the Torah. In Scene 18, Jesus declares that one does not do the will of God by living the Torah.

Endnotes

1. Mark 8:22-26 (Scene 1) is found at the end of Act 4 in our current text; however, it does not fit the Act 4 organization. But it fits perfectly here in the Act 6 organization. Mark 10:1-12 is found here in our current text. That scene does not fit the or-ganization of Act 6; therefore, we know that a scribe inserted it.

2. The opening sentence of the Gospel: "The beginning of the gospel of Jesus Christ, the son of God" does not fit the structure of Scene 1. Further, Mark later calls Jesus' message, the "gospel of God," not the "gospel of Jesus Christ." And he does not address Jesus as "Jesus Christ." Thus, probably this Preface was inserted by a scribe after Mark completed his Work.

3. *Release:* The Greek word, aphesis, can be translated "release," forgiveness, deliverance, unbind, and in other similar ways. I use "release" because it applies to all the contexts in Mark. Aphesis also related to "aphiēmi" which I also translate as "release."

4. Our current text inserts here: "For they were fisherman." Because those words do not fit the structure, they were probably inserted by an early scribe. Notice also that there is not parallel in Part 2.

5. Our current text inserts here: "And I will make you into fishermen of men." Because those words do not fit the structure, they were probably inserted by an early scribe. Notice also that there is not parallel in Part 2.

6. Our current text reads: "Indeed, in order that you might understand that the son of man has authority to release sins upon the earth." We know that this is an insertion by a copyist after the original was composed because it does not fit the structure and because it is not needed.

7. The verses that make up Scene 12 are out of order. I moved them to Scene 12 because they parallel Scene 7.

8. *Simon:* After Simon is the word "Peter" which seems to be a later insertion.

9. *James:* After James are the words "Boanerges or Sons of Thunder "which seems to be a later insertion.

10. Our current text inserts here :"rather he will come to an end." Because those words do not fit the structure, they were probably inserted by an early scribe.

11. Our current text inserts here: "Because they chattered that he has an unclean spirit." And I will make you into fishermen of men (Mk 3:30)." Because those words do not fit the structure, they were probably inserted by an early scribe.

www.ingramcontent.com/pod-product-compliance
Lightning Source LLC
Chambersburg PA
CBHW060424010526
44118CB00017B/2342